A GIRL NEEDS CASH

GIRL
NEEDS
CASH

Banish the White Knight Myth and
Take Charge of Your Financial Life

JOAN PERRY with
DOLORES BARCLAY

TIMES BUSINESS

RANDOM HOUSE

In a number of cases, names and identifying details have been changed in order to protect the privacy of friends, business associates, and clients. The following names of people described in the book are fictional: Jana; Marc; Maggie O'Neal; Maggie O'Neal's boss; Maggie O'Neal's mother, Patricia; Maggie O'Neal's roommate; Lynette Atwood and her child Kimberly; Marshall Atwood; Rachel Levine; David Levine; June Mendoza; Steve Mendoza; Sadie Chung; Sadie Chung's broker; Betty Scott; Louise; Helen; Jackie; Karen; Charlie; Bob.

Copyright © 1997 by Joan Perry

All rights reserved under International and Pan-American Copyright Conventions. Published in the United States by Times Books, a division of Random House, Inc., New York, and simultaneously in Canada by Random House of Canada Limited, Toronto.

Library of Congress Cataloging-in-Publication Data

Perry, Joan A., 1951–
A girl needs cash: how to banish the white knight myth and take charge of your financial life / Joan Perry with Dolores Barclay.
p.   cm.
Includes index.
ISBN 0-8129-2840-7
1. Women—Finance, Personal. 2. Young women—Finance, Personal.
3. Finance, Personal.   4. Investments.   I. Barclay, Dolores A.   II. Title.
HG179.P3668   1997
332.024'042—dc21   97-12704

Random House website address: www.randomhouse.com
Printed in the United States of America on acid-free paper
9   8   7   6   5   4   3   2
First Edition

Book design by Mina Greenstein

From birth to age 18, a girl needs good parents. From 18 to 35, she needs good looks. From 35 to 55, she needs a good personality. And from 55 on, a girl needs cash.

—SOPHIE TUCKER

This book is dedicated to:
the next step for all women on the path to freedom—employing money in their lives;
a girl with cash in her hands, love in her heart, and a smile radiating from her soul;
and, most of all for me, this book is dedicated to my parents, Harriet and Anthony Perry, my husband, Ron Lykins, and my sister, Martha Esterline.

ACKNOWLEDGMENTS

From the center of my being I'm truly grateful—

For my angels in heaven—Suzanne Lipsett, Bill McGrane, and Wayne Bartlett.

For my angels on earth—Dolores Barclay, Karl Weber, Betty Rauch, Tony Robbins, Dean McGrane, Linda Chester, Marilyn Muchnick, Sean Lykins, Molly and Katie Esterline, Dana Rowell, Barbara Henricks, Lynn Goldberg, Alejandra Moreno, Eileen Leffler, Katherine Trobbe, and many treasured people whose stories have given me insights into life.

Contents

A GIRL NEEDS CASH

Money: The Last Taboo

Does thinking about giving your money to a stockbroker give
    you the jitters?

Would you rather have a root canal than think about your finan-
    cial life?

Do you sometimes lose sleep over a spending spree?

Are you in danger of becoming a bag lady when you stop work-
    ing?

Do you own an investment or two that you don't fully under-
    stand?

Are you missing the opportunity to double your money every
    five years?

If you answered yes to one or more of these questions, then read
on. This book is for you.

A Girl Needs Cash will dispel the fears and misconceptions you
may have about creating your financial future and will nurture you

to develop strong, sensible money strategies, whether you're just starting out or have already made some headway with investments. It will also help you realize that handling your money is not as challenging as you think, and can be an enjoyable, fascinating journey toward emotional and personal wholeness.

Anyone can successfully manage her money life. It doesn't matter whether you're young or old; married, partnered, or single; divorced or widowed; employed or unemployed; rich or poor. What is important is that you begin.

While I was working on this book, I spent some time in New York City meeting with my publisher. One spring day, as I wandered in and out of galleries and shops on the streets of SoHo, I ran into my friends Jana and Marc. Jana is a social worker and Marc is a doctor. They're both fortyish and enjoy a comfortable lifestyle. They asked me what I was up to, and I replied, "I'm working on a book about successful money strategies for women."

"That could be a short book," Marc quipped. "You just need two sentences: 'Marry someone rich' and 'Get a good lawyer.' " All three of us laughed.

"Problem is," Jana said, "the lawyer gets all the money." Then she turned more serious and said, "Joan, you have no idea how much I need some useful financial information that I can really relate to. At work, I run an entire department. I set budgets and deal with payrolls and expense accounts. But I really don't know enough about my own personal finances. I just hope that Marc doesn't decide to leave me anytime soon."

Jana's story didn't surprise me. In my work in money matters, I've talked to many women over the years who express the same lament.

"You mean you've done nothing to ensure your financial future?" I inquired.

"Nada," she said. "Hey, not many women have—certainly not too many of my friends. When we were kids, we were always told we never could or didn't have to. Then we went to work and spent a lot of time and energy proving ourselves on the job. And now that we've begun to make our mark in just about every profession and area in life, we still don't know what to do about our financial futures."

Jana, like most women, had grown up thinking a certain way. That's "herstory." There's not much we can do about how we've been raised. But if you're ready to begin the journey of how you'll build cash for your future, you're going to need some "rewiring"—you're going to have to change how you envision yourself as a woman and the role money plays in your life.

Helping you explore and, if need be, change your attitudes about money, is a primary focus of *A Girl Needs Cash*. I'm not only going to guide you to some sensible and effective money strategies; I'm also going to encourage you to realize your power as a woman and accept what might seem a revolutionary concept: *You can, you will, and you must have control over your financial life.*

Taking financial control is part of our natural evolution and the last step in our liberation as women. The freedom we enjoy today came in stages: from education to the vote to control of our health to increased employment opportunities to more power in our relationships. Most of us have gone to work, and some of us have made a lot of money in these changing times; others have remained at home, working in concert with a partner to raise families and run households. In either case, today's generation of women has greater freedom and opportunity than previous ones. But have we made this new freedom work for us? The truth is, regardless of age, occupation, marital status, or future promise, we must all go to the next level and actively develop our financial well-being.

It's not that women consider their financial lives unimportant. Nor do they purposely shirk responsibility. But centuries of cultural biases, misconceptions, and fears conspire to hold us back. We are not *supposed* to be interested or involved in money matters; thus many of us are unprepared to tackle the issue and we put it out of our minds.

Certainly, like so many passages in life, taking charge of your financial life is a path to new challenges. (Plenty of men are intimidated about money matters, too—even if they're too macho to admit it.) But investing is also one of the most enjoyable things you'll ever do. Watching your money work for you is a singular treat, one that can give you pleasure as it raises the quality of your life. How can you envision financial opportunity? Begin by understanding and dumping the influences that keep you from this very important stage in the cycle of life.

At stake is a secure future for yourself and your family. The bottom line—for you and me and everyone—is that you will probably have to manage a large sum of money—perhaps millions—by the time you stop working if you hope to live as well as, if not better than, you did during your working years. So if you don't begin the process of investing now, you can't be certain of a healthy—and happy—financial future.

In the pages that follow, I'm going to introduce you to some of my clients, friends, and associates whose lives and money matters just might mirror your own. I'll also share my personal investment and professional experiences with you. I've learned a lot from them, and perhaps you might avoid some of my trials and tribulations.

Thinking back to my early life, I can see that it was in athletics that I honed the competitive skills I later needed to survive as a woman in the investment banking world of Wall Street. I spent my childhood competing in diving and swimming meets, and in the 1960s, I even won Illinois state diving championships. Those competitions provided valuable life lessons for the working world—how to hang in there, how to move toward what I wanted to achieve, and how to make it happen. Competition taught me that nothing was really out of my reach; all I had to do was focus and rely on my own effort and skills, not someone else's. And I learned to compete not only against others but also against myself, to strive always to improve the results I achieved. That spirit toughened me for the investment world, where only one word seemed to matter: *win*.

After graduating from Denison University, I entered business school to earn my MBA (Master of Business Administration). It was the early 1970s, and I was one of just five women in my class at the Owen Graduate School of Management at Vanderbilt University in

Nashville, Tennessee. Several of us were athletes who had developed a thick skin from putting ourselves out there in public to test our skills. I was proud of myself and my female classmates, and certain I had what it took to compete, advance, and prosper in the dogfight that was business as usual on Wall Street. I was also very curious about what I could learn.

My self-confidence and my excitement at being in the female vanguard seemed well placed at first. My career on Wall Street progressed as I'd hoped and planned. Within a decade, I had established the first female-owned municipal bond brokerage firm in the United States. My business and my life were exciting, profitable, and full of possibilities. I did all the things smart, successful, dynamic young professionals did: I bought a car and a wonderful house, I wore lots of great clothes, and I was dating a delightful man, who was charming and who had made big money.

Still, something was wrong with this picture.

Trouble was, despite my success as an investment banker, I didn't have a whole lot of cash. I had the investments in my business, but no real personal investments. And to keep up with all my various lifestyle choices—and the credit card debt they created—I was living on cash flow virtually month by month. As a result, I was financially and emotionally insecure. I was also, at a gut level, angry that, despite working hard and gaining a lot of professional skills, I didn't feel safe or affluent because I was basically starting over each month. There was pain, frustration, and fear, because I knew that without any real investments, I was close to the brink. I didn't choose to cut back because I was wedded to my lifestyle.

But what did I have to complain about? I was doing what I had always imagined myself doing, and having a terrific time. Until, in the kindest way possible, the man I had been dating told me it was over between us. He walked out of my life, and the bottom fell out of my world.

The real shock wasn't that this man left me. It was what I discovered about myself after he was gone. For all my apparent independence and competitive edge, for all my business training and knowledge of how money can bring security, for all my financial savvy . . . I suddenly felt that the man who was going to *take care of my long-term financial future* had ridden off into the sunset, leaving me completely—intolerably!—on my own.

I was left with a horrible feeling in my stomach. Suddenly, I realized that I was flying alone without a safety net. I was living month by month, and unless I got it together, I was always going to live this way. Nobody was there to work out a plan for me; if I were to have any sort of financial future, I was going to have to make one for myself. It was fear and insecurity and self-doubt that were making my stomach do somersaults, and I didn't like that feeling at all.

I realized that certain beliefs were handicapping me—beliefs I'd sheltered so deeply that I hadn't even realized I had them. I had been harboring a destructive, self-deprecating fantasy: This man— and, I guess, *any* man who entered my life on an intimate level— was going to take care of me and my financial security. I was a victim of the "White Knight Syndrome."

Once this realization hit me, I took to the problem like a terrier to a bone. Curious about where I stood, I began to ask my female colleagues in the brokerage world and elsewhere what they were doing about their financial futures. I found an epidemic of the White Knight Syndrome, and a weird repetition of my own circumstances: house, car, credit card debt, and virtually no investments.

Even more surprising were the answers I elicited from my male colleagues on Wall Street. For the most part, they, too, admitted to the house-car-credit-card triangle. In the lives of these financial professionals, investing seemed to be way down the list of personal priorities. Their firms were bringing in all kinds of financial experts and economists to make presentations that gave them an accurate picture of the global scene, and I'd assumed that, unlike me, they were putting their growing sophistication to use in developing their personal portfolios. But at home, after working hours, these folks, like me, were right there with the rest of the population, living in the moment and preparing very little, if at all, for the day when their earning years would be changing.

What was going on?

I concluded that the combination of our youth, our culture, our crazy work pace, and our single-minded competitiveness was making us believe—perhaps unconsciously—either that we'd keep earning forever, or that we'd never live long enough to have to worry about the days when we'd no longer be working.

When we start working, many of us use our first paychecks—which seem so big at the time—to buy an array of goodies: cars, stereos, computers, clothes, jewelry, sporting goods, CDs, books, videos. And advertisers and retailers, who try to make us believe that we'll have a good life if we buy their products, constantly nudge us to keep spending. But how often do you see commercials or ads telling you about the joys of keeping some of your money and building your own wealth?

Because we're young, we feel invincible. We naively believe we don't have to squirrel away anything for the future because "there's plenty of time." And so we put off engaging in our own financial life and instead indulge our whims.

Later, after we've accumulated all the toys and luxuries we can fit into our homes or our lives, we get caught up in the whirligig of career and continue to delay making any real inroads toward building our financial security. Finally, when we become "women of a certain age," we think it's too late to begin, and so we don't bother.

Once I realized how my attitudes stood in the way of my financial progress, and that I had to take action, I started to wise up. Because of the business I was in, I knew how to make investments work for me; the challenge was to slow down long enough to set them up. So I devoted time to thinking about my life and where I wanted to be five, ten, twenty, and thirty years from now. I developed an investment philosophy grounded in the basics of financial life, along with a personal investment strategy designed to generate a steadily producing, low-maintenance "Money Machine" in order to yield the cash I'd need down the line when I was ready to ease out of working. This didn't happen overnight. It took several years of careful planning, assessing, and soul-searching.

Finally, with my personal life plans in place and working, I began Take Charge Financial!—a securities-brokerage, financial-advisory, and insurance-licensed firm with a mission. The thrust of my company is to sort out the best ways in the universe of financial options for people to take charge of their money lives and to build the wealth they'll need for *their* futures—and not, as is the unspoken rule on Wall Street, for their brokers' firms.

A Girl Needs Cash draws on my experience as both a recovered White Knight Syndrome sufferer and a client-oriented coach to illustrate the thinking and strategies that have served me and my clients well. It explains how to create a vibrant Money Machine to secure your nonworking future.

The book is short and direct because, although investment professionals love to mystify their profession, the principles of sound investment are clear and direct. But "clear and direct" in no way implies "unimportant." The information and insights you'll find here can mean the difference between poverty and security in your future.

So read this book for a little first aid for your spirit and soul and also your wealth. I think you'll find that if you slow down, take a few deep breaths, and let *A Girl Needs Cash* do its work, the terrible feeling you have in your stomach, the thumping you have at your temples, or the emptiness you feel when you think about your financial future will disappear—and you'll sense new strength in your power as a woman living in the best of times.

1

Hot-Tub Logic:
Embracing Our Money Lives

Women Talking Money
Financial Evolution
The Wheel of Life
Positive Moneymaking
Cash for Your Financial Future!

WOMEN TALKING MONEY

It was an early winter day in Tecate, Mexico, the hour when late afternoon meets early evening in a chilly embrace. It was a perfect time to snuggle on the sofa in front of a cedar fire or slip into a warm woolen sweater to stroll through the tangle of thyme, rosemary, and laurel bushes. Or you could do what I did that particular day: slide into the welcoming warmth of a hot tub.

I was at Rancho La Puerta, a retreat nestled high in the Mexican sierra, easing my mind and body into healthier shape after a challenging year. I was also scheduled to speak at an after-dinner program later that week about women and their money—a topic I'd been thinking a lot about for some time.

Now I found myself sitting naked with six other women in a large outdoor tub, unwinding from an exercise-laden day of hiking, stretching, tennis, aerobics, and yoga. We were a friendly, relaxed bunch who easily enjoyed one another's conversation in the warmth of the tub. Although from different parts of the country and with different backgrounds, we had something in common—we were all reflecting on how our lives could be more comfortable and on our sense of being more settled. The Ranch, as we fondly called the Mexican retreat, offered a blissful setting for that type of contemplation. It was also a place that encouraged our friendship and made the sharing of experiences and intimacies an enjoyable and cozy pursuit.

As we came to know one another, I mentioned what had brought me to the Ranch, and the conversation quickly turned to money. It's not an easy topic for most people to talk about; our dreams, desires, and self-worth are so caught up with money that most people consider it an inappropriate topic for open discussion, the way sex and religion used to be. But in the easy surroundings of the Ranch, far from the constraints and pressures of our daily lives, my companions and I found ourselves sharing feelings we otherwise would have concealed.

We gradually discovered some remarkable similarities when it came to feelings about money. A couple of the women were fairly savvy and were working toward some long-range financial goals; others were confused or frustrated about their financial well-being.

One twenty-five-year-old in the group hadn't saved a dime and was slogging her way through credit card hell, wondering how she got there and if she'd ever find a way out. She would have peace of mind, she said, if she could conquer her finances. Another woman, who was struggling with a nasty divorce, readily agreed and quickly added that she'd find a little relief from financial stress if she could invest for her future and know that she'd have enough money to support herself and her child comfortably.

"That would be my dream come true," she said, sighing. "To me, investing is freedom."

Her remark shook me from my hot-tub haze, but in no way lessened my mellow mood. I'm very curious about a woman's point of view, especially when it comes to financial matters. Many of my clients are women, and they view the money in their lives a lot differently than men do. Besides, I consider investing to be more than merely a way to collect cash. To me, investing is a way to nurture our souls and our lives.

"You know, she's right. How we relate to money directly affects other aspects of our lives," I said. "This is part of what I'll be talking about later this week."

My companions seemed to welcome a forum in which they could freely talk about money matters. And the outdoors, with the sun setting behind the mountains and the breeze carrying the sweet scent of rosemary, offered an idyllic setting for us to sift through our financial points of view. For the most part, the women were remarkably free, and our chat soon began to churn as much as the water in the tub.

For many people, though, money is a tough topic to confront. Even *talking* about money can be intimidating. In a 1995 survey by Roper Starch Worldwide, Inc., only 26 out of 1,043 women polled said they talk about investing and finance with their family and friends and 16 percent said they regularly read articles about the topic. The percentage for men was only slightly higher. Even more alarming, another Roper Starch survey in 1996 found that only 47 percent of 1,002 women aged eighteen and older saved regularly for their future years.

It warmed me to see that these women were finally beginning to talk about money, which is part of everyone's weave of life, like it or not. Silence is often shattered once you realize that your experiences—and your challenges—are universal.

But as essential to our well-being as money is, few people share their intimate experiences, joys, or confusion about money—even with their closest friends or loved ones. Most people have no problem at all talking about their jobs, their families, or even sex. But money is another matter.

Think about it. When was the last time you went to lunch with your best friend and talked about money? No, not men! Money!

Not your job, family, sex, or shopping, but money? When was the last time you discussed choices for your financial future, or how you'll be living ten, twenty, or thirty years from now? Will you be a bag lady? Or will you be a well-set-up, comfortable, and secure woman? What strategies will work best to create a healthy financial future?

Many women have never considered these questions, partly because most of us grew up in a society that did not expect or invite women to participate in financial affairs; money is our last taboo.

But remember—sex got better once we started talking about it freely from our perspective as women, and sharing our experiences and problems. When we did, we were thrilled to discover how much we had in common. The worries, fears, desires, and fantasies we'd harbored in secret turned out to be universal. And armed with this knowledge, we were able to take back control of our sexual lives from the "experts"—the male doctors and authority figures we used to listen to. The result was liberating: Most of us discovered a healthier, more rewarding way to think about and enjoy sex.

The same can be true for money. And the good news is, some women are beginning to discover that not only can we discuss money, but we can also actively direct this important aspect of our lives.

I shared that notion with my tub mates, who I'd discovered were smart, educated, and all very good at what they did in life. Yet it became clear that some of them had reached adulthood knowing next to nothing about the personal aspects of money and how to make it grow. As we relaxed and talked, they shared their stories.

Maggie O'Neal

Crimson-haired Maggie O'Neal is a twenty-five-year-old photographer's assistant who looks even younger than her age and has a splash of freckles across her nose. Maggie earns $18,000 a year, and spares her cash by sharing an apartment with another young woman in downtown New Orleans. Unfortunately, she loves the smell of burning money and will yield to her indulgences in a minute—like the $200 boots she recently bought that almost ate up an entire paycheck. But she resents the intrusion of basic responsibilities, like rent, telephone bills, and credit card statements.

Maybe it's because as a child growing up in North Carolina, Maggie didn't have to work for anything. She never had a summer job (it was so much more fun to spend July and August hanging out with the lifeguards at the beach), and her only household responsibility was to occasionally clean her room. When she went off to study photography at Duke University, her parents gave her a checking account: They put money in, she took it out—and she was constantly overdrawn.

Today, Maggie's parents continue to coddle their daughter by sometimes paying her bills. Each month, Maggie struggles to figure out how to pay her share of the rent and at least part of her ever-mushrooming credit card debt. I wondered how Maggie could afford her trip to the Ranch. Maggie volunteered the answer: It was a twenty-fifth-birthday present from her mom. Some months, if her parents won't help her pay the bills by giving her a loan (really a gift, since Maggie never pays it back), she asks her boss for an advance on her paycheck.

Linette Atwood

Linette Atwood is a thirty-eight-year-old New York marketing specialist and the mother of a ten-year-old girl. She is an attractive, athletic woman who boasts a buff body, elegantly braided hair, and chiseled cheeks. People sometimes mistake Linette for Angela Bassett, the movie star; this makes Linette feel both embarrassed and flattered. Sadly, she finds it hard to accept compliments. Linette has a low opinion of herself these days, especially after the breakup of her marriage. She and Marshall recently separated, and the divorce papers have just been filed.

Linette is a successful businesswoman—she makes about $50,000 a year—and Marshall earns considerably more as vice president of a magazine chain. How much, Linette doesn't exactly know. The couple's financial picture isn't clear to Linette because she left money matters up to Marshall. She deposited paychecks in their joint checking account and left balancing the checkbook to her husband. Marshall paid all the bills and made all the investments. Linette trusted him and never seemed to have any reason to question what he did. (And with Marshall's temper, she wouldn't have felt comfortable, anyway. Whenever she tried to discuss money, he became agitated.) Now that they've separated and their finances are gradually being disentangled, Linette is learning where their money has been going. The picture isn't a pretty one. Marshall frittered away much of their money buying expensive "toys," such as the $6,000 stereo system and the top-of-the-line gym equipment he had to have to furnish their beach house in the Hamptons. Even worse, Marshall dropped thousands of dollars on the Caribbean vacations he took with the twenty-four-year-old model with whom he'd been having an affair. Investments? The bank and brokerage accounts turned out to be shockingly small.

Linette was devastated, and her pride, enthusiasm, and self-esteem plunged to the cellar. Her future is uncertain, and she has spent many nights awake brooding about how her daughter will be able to attend college. She's been visiting the Ranch for the past four years, and she hopes that a time of quiet reflection and meditation in a tranquil setting she loves will help heal her wounds and, maybe, give her some fresh insights into how to handle her unhappy situation.

Rachel Levine

Rachel Levine, a thirty-year-old assistant curator at a Dallas art museum, is a lusciously full-figured woman with short-cropped, dark brown hair that frames her soft blue eyes. She earns $30,000 a year. She and her husband, David, a contractor whose annual income is $45,000, live in an old, run-down ranch house they purchased for $60,000, intending to restore it. Their dream is to renovate the house and sell it for a handsome profit. They devote their weekends to fix-up projects, and they've been able to do much of the work themselves. But it's a slow process: The front hall and two bedrooms are done, but the rest of the house is in many different stages of rebuilding. Just before coming to the Ranch, Rachel and David turned a closet into a bathroom.

An excellent cook, Rachel loves to entertain. She often invites friends over to help with renovation projects and serves elaborate dinners as a reward. She and David hope to start a family, but they haven't found the time to seriously talk it over. That's because when they aren't working around the house or going to their individual jobs, they are playing tennis, scouring yard sales for antique fixtures and furniture, and chumming around with friends.

The Levines are frugal with their household expenses, but the expenses for building supplies and the occasional professional helper—an electrician to rewire the house, for example—add up. Rachel started an individual retirement account (IRA) when she was twenty-four, and she has $10,000 saved in a joint money market account with David. But she confesses to feeling uneasy about her investments, which have been growing too slowly for comfort. And she finds herself bleeding her savings little by little in order to pay off credit card debts.

June Mendoza

June Mendoza is a fifty-year-old Michigan housewife. She's a tall, handsome woman who wears her age gracefully: a few fine wrinkles crease the corners of her bright, chocolate brown eyes; her graying hair loops into a casual bun. June, who never entered the workforce, married Steve thirty years ago, the day after her graduation from junior college. He works for a pharmaceutical firm and earns about $55,000 a year, plus bonuses.

June and Steve have three children. The oldest, Mary, lives in California. She's married with a three-year-old son. The middle child, Steve Jr., works in Seattle as a deejay at a rock 'n' roll club.

The youngest, Ellie, is twenty years old. She recently moved into her own apartment in Madison Heights, just a few miles from her parents.

June has devoted the past few years to Ellie, who has an eating disorder and other emotional problems. Ellie is doing better these days—family therapy with a gifted counselor has been a huge help—but the cost of her care has eroded the family's savings. (Steve's company switched their medical insurance to an HMO [health maintenance organization] four years ago, and somehow the benefits for psychological help have never been quite enough since then.) June doesn't know the details because, as Linette did, she leaves all financial matters to her husband.

Now that Ellie is working and beginning to take care of herself, June is able to focus on her own life for the first time since her marriage. It's a welcome treat to be able to think about her own interests, needs, and desires. Yet, paradoxically, she is finding life stressful, too. It used to be hectic and demanding, but predictable. Now she's wondering where to channel her energy. And in the back of her mind, she wonders, too, whether Steve has made the right money decisions that will give them the freedom to travel and have adventures after all their years of hard work. But for June, to consider questioning Steve's judgment in money matters would be disturbing—almost more disturbing for June than for Steve. After so many years of allowing Steve to handle their affairs alone, why make waves now—and possibly trouble the outward calm of their happy marriage?

Sadie Chung

Sadie Chung is a petite fifty-nine-year-old woman with stylishly bobbed ebony hair and the taut body of a woman twenty years her junior. As she sat in the hot tub, though, I noticed a slight puffiness to her face. Worry lines creased her brow. For a decade, she lived in Hong Kong with her investment-banker husband while working as a travel writer. Then he was transferred to Boston, where they lived until his death four years ago. Sadie still writes poetry and short fiction (her stories about life in China appear frequently in magazines), and she is occasionally a guest on TV talk shows.

From her husband, Sadie inherited $1.5 million in stocks, bonds, annuities, and insurance, plus some real estate. From her writing and other activities, she earns anywhere from $40,000 to $150,000 a year, depending on sales of her writing and the number of speaking engagements she accepts, although she's beginning to slow down. Eventually, she hopes to rechannel her energies toward her literacy volunteer work with youngsters in the Roxbury area of Boston.

Sadie's financial life allows her to live comfortably, yet she's confused and overwhelmed by the cornucopia of investments her husband left behind. She finds it difficult to keep track of everything she owns, and she feels that her husband's longtime broker (and sometime fishing buddy) is both intimidating and condescending. This irritates and offends her, but she isn't sure what to do about it.

Betty Scott

The last of the women is Betty Scott, a forty-two-year-old who lives in San Francisco. Betty earns $76,000 a year as a lawyer for a firm that specializes in environmental issues. An energetic blonde with an equally energetic personality, Betty has devoted her life to her career. Building her reputation, growing her client list, and making money have been the center of her universe, and everything else has been either pushed to the margins or simply put on hold, including some of the basic things on which her contemporaries have focused: settling down with a partner and establishing roots. The one special thing she owns is a Victorian house, which she recently bought and which she plans to renovate.

Even handling the money she's earned is merely a footnote in Betty's increasingly demanding professional life. She has an IRA (because it was easy and convenient to open), a 401(k) plan (which was set up by her firm), and a stash of cash in her checking account.

She wants to buy some stock—she hears the chatter at dinner parties about how dynamic the markets have been—but hasn't found the time to figure out exactly which ones.

"Look, this is not tough stuff," I offered the group.

"Oh, yeah, right," Maggie interjected.

"No, really," I continued. "It's a matter of having some strategies, following through with them, and rearranging some old thinking regarding money matters. And the same basic principles of investing apply no matter where you are in your financial life. Anyone can invest, with any amount of money—and you can learn what it takes to have wise investing strategies."

"Oh, I'm sure that's interesting, but I don't need any of that," June said with a touch of disinterest. "I've got him."

"Him?" I asked, somewhat perplexed.

"Um, yes. My husband. He has things under control," June responded. "Maybe someday I'll want to learn about investing, but right now, I'm off for a massage." She climbed out of the tub, quickly slipped into her robe, and hastily padded away.

"Well, I'm not afraid to admit that I *do* need to hear about this stuff," Betty remarked. "I'm so glad you'll be speaking. I'll be right there in the front row. You know, I've been meaning to talk to someone like you. I'll be honest—I've never really thought beyond today because I'm too busy with work. I have the feeling that my money ought to be working for me, too."

"Yes, that's important, dear," Sadie offered.

"Well, I guess I'm just zoned out by it all," Maggie admitted.

Linette chimed in with a knowing laugh. "You're not alone," she said. "I handle million-dollar accounts with some of the world's biggest corporations, but I don't know an annuity from a mutual fund. I really feel dumb."

"Linette, I think you're being too hard on yourself. If you ask around—talk to other women—I think you'll discover that very few of them know all that much about investing. Truth is, we haven't been taught," Rachel said in a soothing, quiet voice.

"That's very true," Sadie said. "It took me years to realize that my brother learned things I didn't as a child. Maybe that's why he was always more financially aggressive than me. In my day, that was true with most women."

"Amen," Linette said. "No one ever talked to me about my finances when I was growing up. And you know something? I don't think I ever really talked about money with my girlfriends. Why have we waited so long to discuss this? Now I'm embarrassed to say I've done very little with my money."

"Oh, please don't be embarrassed," I said. "Many of us have done very little. Lots of women are just beginning to learn about money matters. You're actually ahead of the curve because you're beginning to raise questions."

"Unfortunately, it looks like June isn't interested," Rachel said.

"Right now I guess she's being led by some out-of-date thinking," I suggested. "She seems to think that having a husband to handle her money will solve everything. Perhaps she'll be open to discussion at another time in her life. Let's hope so. But the important thing for you, for all women, really, is to envision a financial future and to take steps toward it. Hey, we don't want to be bag ladies after leading such productive lives, do we?" I said.

"Whoa! Homeless. No way," said Maggie. She lifted herself out of the water, wrapped a robe around her body, and sat on the tiled edge of the tub, her feet dangling in the water. She was a scarlet vision, her freckled skin reddened from the heat.

"But things *are* a little rough right now," she admitted.

"Rough how? Paying bills?" Betty asked.

"Yeah. I'm in hock. Big time," Maggie replied. "The worse thing is that I feel paralyzed. I don't know how to get out from under, let alone invest. What money I have, I feed to Visa and MasterCard."

"That's the worst feeling," said Rachel. "I remember those days well. Right after college, when I first started working, I was constantly strapped. But then I found another job that paid more, and I promised myself that I'd never again be so desperate. After that, I saved some money and began buying penny stocks—you know, those stocks that sell for a dollar or two. My first one was Sunshine Mines, and I made a little money."

"So do you still use your credit cards?" Maggie asked.

"Yes. Very, very carefully." Rachel laughed. "And we try to pay off the entire balance each month. But it's still not easy. Most of the cash my husband and I make goes back into work around our house."

"You're fixing up an old house?" Betty said. "I just bought one of those old Victorians. It needs some work, but not much. Mostly restoration. I'm having so much fun peeling back wallpaper and chipping off paint to find old brick. You guys must be having a ball."

"Ours is a carpenter's nightmare," Rachel replied with a grin. "Here, feel my hand." She stretched across the tub and exposed the layer of calluses on her palm.

"So almost all of your money is tied up in the house?" I asked Rachel.

"Just about," she replied. "Why? That's not a good idea?"

"Let's talk later—your home is not really an investment because it's not going to pay you cash in the future," I said.

"My husband and I do have some questions about how we're using our money, and right now, we're asking ourselves if we have enough cash left over to move on to really 'important' investments," Rachel said.

"I hear the lawyers in my office talking about more sophisticated approaches for their money, and some of it sounds good," said Betty. "Problem is, it seems like there are so many options, and I'm not the kind of person who blindly jumps into things."

"How about somebody like me? . . . Where do I start?" Maggie asked. "I'm not like the rest of you guys. I don't have any money to invest."

"Believe it or not, you do, Maggie," I said. "You'd be surprised how you're being influenced to spend your money right now instead of holding on to it."

The questions, comments, and concerns of these women are universal. I hear similar ones from clients and others who are stretching their investment muscles. All too often, women feel bewildered by money matters and wrongly assume solutions will be difficult. Believe it or not, as you will learn in this book, the answers and approaches are within your reach.

I shifted around in the tub as an eager wind carried a slight chill and the cleansing fragrance of rosemary from a nearby bush. Ah, such sweetness. I was grateful that my life could embrace this simplicity. I felt happy to be with these women in such a joyful environment.

I hoisted myself from the tub before I became a human prune, bundled myself in a soft, thick terry robe, and took a long hard drink from my water bottle. The other women also began climbing out of the gurgling pool, and we ambled back to the locker room to shower and crawl into our sweats and sweaters. We had had such camaraderie in the hot tub and were just getting started in our conversation, so we decided to continue over dinner. We chose a large round table in the retreat's dining room near an open hearth with a crackling fire. After a while, June joined us when she spotted the big friendly table. She looked great, her cheeks rosy from her massage, a lift in her step.

FINANCIAL EVOLUTION

"You know, taking care of your financial self is just as important as nourishing your body," I said, as we began eating a spicy lentil soup.

Linette got the drift. "Women need to know more about their financial care, just as we learned more about our bodies and our health a decade ago and took charge," the marketing expert said. Linette had a way of zeroing in on a target and getting to the nub— as long as it wasn't her life.

She was correct in her assessment of women and money. Unfortunately, not many women are actively engaged in their financial life. That's because, as Rachel noted back at the hot tub, no one teaches us—not at home and not at school.

Think about your own background for a minute. Did your father or mother expose you to the mysteries and realities of fiscal responsibility—discuss the importance of investing or how to plan for your nonworking years? Did your parents encourage you to save pennies, nickels, and dimes at an early age? Did your parents—or teachers—give you the skinny on how to stay out of debt, pay your bills, and meet other financial responsibilities?

I put these very same questions to the women at the table, and only Betty, Rachel, and Sadie claimed to have developed a slight money sense at a young age.

"Whenever we went shopping, my mother would give me the money to pay the cashier. She used to tell me that I had to learn the value of a dollar," Sadie said. "But she never told me how to earn that dollar and put it away and watch it expand."

"I had a piggy bank—actually, it was a poodle," Betty said. "My mom told me to put all my coins in there 'for a rainy day.' Of course, whenever it rained, I'd take out the money and buy some ice cream or go to a movie!" Everyone laughed.

"My parents didn't speak to me about money until I got my first after-school job as a teenager," Rachel said. "Then all they said was to open a savings account. I did, and I used it to pay for a trip to visit my sister in Baltimore. What about you, Joan? How did you learn about money?"

That was a good question—one I'd thought a great deal about and could readily answer.

"It took me years to fully understand and respect the power of money—and my power as a woman—and learn how to develop strategies for my personal money growth and health," I said.

"I first learned about the importance of cash when I was nine years old. It was then that I ventured into my first moneymaking enterprise, running a 'restaurant' with a gaggle of other neighborhood kids in the backyard of a friend's house in Decatur, Illinois. My friends and I made macaroni and cheese and hot dogs using food our moms had bought, and we sold the snacks to other kids and a few adults. On a good weekend, we could earn as much as $25. Believe me, we carefully counted those nickels and dimes and quarters! We divided our bounty, and I stowed away my share in a shoe box. I could buy whatever I wanted with my shoe-box stash, but what I most enjoyed was watching that cardboard chest fill up with cash. I knew nothing of investing back then, and so it never occurred to me that I could earn money on my money."

"When did you learn about investing?" Maggie asked, working on a salad of young greens.

"That happened a short while later, when my parents encouraged me to open a savings account at the local bank," I said, smiling at the memory. "I remember that treasured little blue passbook and how I would watch the column of handwritten numbers grow every time I went into the bank to collect my interest."

"*Handwritten* numbers?" Maggie echoed in disbelief.

"Yes. This was a small bank in a small town," I replied. "Anyway, when I was twelve, my father gave me my own checking account. That was a radical move for the late 1960s. Even today, a seventh-grader with a personal checking account is a bit unusual. What makes it even more unusual, looking back, is that at the time, my mother didn't have her own checking account—she shared my father's account. It was a peculiar double standard.

"But my father wanted to teach me fiscal responsibility. And regardless of motive, his gesture did me a great service. To begin with, being one of the few kids in junior high school with a checkbook really enhanced my self-esteem. Second, as my dad had hoped, handling a checking account taught me a lot about responsibility. With my little account, which my father launched with a hefty fifty bucks, I was cautious and calculating. Each week, I looked forward to depositing my allowance and the money I earned from baby-sitting, and I happily balanced my checkbook each month, feeling oh-so-grown-up. Best of all, I had a sense that I could make some money choices—simple ones, such as what I wanted to buy for lunch, the kinds of pens and notebooks I should get, and how much I should keep in my account.

"At that point in my life, I had no idea that money could grow and vastly expand if you left it alone and didn't spend it but invested it instead. But investing wasn't the idea; collecting was. I liked to accumulate cash so I could spend it. As a kid, I worked a lot, usually as a baby-sitter or a lifeguard, just so I could fatten my account. I always had money when I was young. So I was very lucky. My parents gave me a strong work ethic, and my father gave me an early taste of financial responsibility.

"More to the point, I found tremendous joy just by being in control. I had watched my mother struggle over money issues when I was a child. I remember how frustrated she was at times when we went shopping in St. Louis and she didn't have enough money to buy the things she wanted. That convinced me that I wanted to be in a position to buy what I craved and not have to ask someone else—namely a man—to purchase it for me. After all, how were the men in my life going to understand that a woman needs a different pair of shoes—and the right color—to match each outfit?

"Later, my mother went to work, successfully launching her own travel agency and travel school. I look back on that now as one of the happiest days of my life, because she became much happier once she had some control over money matters. And I learned that having some money of my own was essential to my freedom as a woman. That's the underlying importance of being financially sound: knowing that you'll have a fruitful financial future. It's as basic as being physically and spiritually healthy, because—let's face it—cash and what to do with it are necessities of modern living and the wellspring of spiritual, physical, and mental health."

The women wanted to hear more, so I introduced them to the "Wheel of Life."

THE WHEEL OF LIFE

How we feel about money, how we deal with it, and how it impacts our lives are directly related to our overall well-being. Money is one spoke in the Wheel of Life. Imagine a large bicycle with a huge front wheel and a tiny back one, the old-fashioned kind of bicycle that was so popular in the late nineteenth century. Now picture yourself sitting atop that gigantic front wheel. Without good balance, it's hard to stay on; and without a solid wheel, you'll surely take a spill. Now look more closely at the wheel. It has seven spokes, representing the seven main areas of our lives:

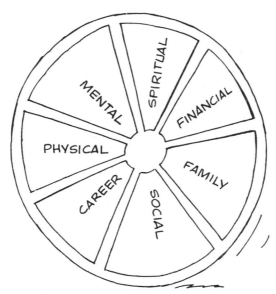

No one spoke is more important than another, and the key to good living is to maintain good balance among them all. You must have good strategies in all seven areas, and some awareness. Otherwise, your Wheel of Life simply won't roll along without bumps and thumps, which may give you a nasty fall.

So you'll want to nurture your financial life, just as you do your health, your family, your career, and everything else that keeps you pumping.

Many women are neglecting this important spoke in their Wheel of Life. One reason is that traditionally, we've allowed someone else to take care of our financial life for us: a parent, a partner, a boyfriend, a husband, or even a broker, a banker, or some other adviser. That's where June is right now, and where Linette used to be. But ignoring our financial well-being or hoping someone else will take care of it hinders self-fulfillment; no one else can pedal your bicycle for you. And, because money issues often get tied up with our self-esteem and peace of mind, when you're not knowledgeable about, and in charge of, your finances, sooner or later your emotional and mental health begin to suffer.

"I guess that's what's happening in my life right now," said Maggie. "I'm so on edge most of the time because I'm so stressed about money. Let me tell you, finding a way out of the hole I've dug seems impossible. What really troubles me is that sometimes I get migraines."

"What a difficult place to be—drags down your self-esteem, too," Sadie said gently.

"That's for sure. And I'm a little ashamed to be taking money from my parents," Maggie confessed. "You know, I've been listening to you guys, and you have no idea how much you're helping me. You see, I've never really been on my own. I guess that, deep down, I never even thought of being responsible for myself. My parents have always been there—and I hoped I'd meet some rich wonderful guy and he'd take over."

But the reality—as Maggie is slowly coming to grasp—is that as women, we have sole responsibility for our financial well-being, whether we're single, married, divorced, widowed, or partnered. I can't emphasize that point enough.

POSITIVE MONEYMAKING

Linette and Betty are at the top of their professions. They reflect how women have become proven performers in today's business world by ascending the career ladder and succeeding. And if corporate America still doesn't fully embrace us and recognize and reward our accomplishments, we've also done well at striking out on our own, creating and managing our own businesses.

Not surprisingly, independent businesswomen tend to have a firmer grasp of money matters than most other women. A 1996 Roper Starch study bears this out: Most female business owners (51 percent) manage their own finances; however, less than half (37 percent) of women in general do so.

Still, too many women are at great financial risk. Even those who have successful corporate or entrepreneurial careers often don't make the most of their money by actively growing their wealth. It's like so many athletes and rock stars, who, like morning glories, blossom overnight, only to lose it all before the next sunrise—they make a lot of money and spend it just as fast, ending up with little to show for their success when their careers are over.

But see what happens when you do make money work for you. A good example is Oprah Winfrey, the popular talk-show host, who is one of the best-known and most admired women in the world. For the past few years, Oprah has been listed in *Forbes* magazine as one of the four hundred richest people in America. Worth more than $415 million, Oprah is a woman who didn't marry into or inherit her wealth. She earned it.

Not every TV star makes the *Forbes* list. How did Oprah leverage her success as an entertainer into significant long-lasting wealth? Not only did she establish a financial empire based on her lucrative television contracts, but she also founded and built her own production company, Harpo, to further multiply her money and extend its reach.

Most admirably, Oprah has used her money to create value for society. For example, she donated $750,000 to her alma mater, Tennessee State University, to set up a scholarship fund—her donation was one of the largest contributions in the school's history. Furthermore, she didn't just sign the check and split. She followed up by personally contacting the students who received the scholarships and by encouraging them to do well in their studies. That's what positive moneymaking is all about—serving yourself and benefiting the lives of others.

This opportunity isn't available only to the rich and famous. Here's a story about a woman I know in New York—I'll call her Louise. Louise worked her way through college while helping to support her five brothers and sisters. She went into advertising, and, after a number of years of diligent work, became a successful, highly respected executive at a New York agency. By nurturing her financial life, Louise managed to invest part of her salary, and with the help of some effective strategies, she grew her savings into a few hundred thousand dollars.

This nest egg allowed Louise to dramatically change her life. Because of the income from her investments, Louise was able to quit her advertising job and devote herself full-time to volunteer work at a facility for children with AIDS. Now, every time I see Louise, she's all aglow, delighted with her good fortune—that she can choose the way she wants to spend her time.

Another woman I knew—I'll call her Helen—started a garden in her backyard in a small Georgia town. She marketed her crop of onions, garlic, and leeks from a roadside stand in front of her house. Her vegetables were so good that the business grew steadily. Soon, Helen was able to afford a larger plot of land for her produce, especially her sweet Vidalia onions, which people began to recommend to their friends. Now she does a thriving mail-order business in this delicious vegetable, and lots of people around the country enjoy her tasty treat.

But positive moneymaking eludes many of us. Why? Because, as the old saying goes, "Most people major in the minor things in life, and minor in the major things in life." They often ignore key elements in their lives, throwing their Wheel of Life out of balance.

If you're especially good at sports, then perhaps you concentrate on this aspect of your life while overlooking your family or finances. Rachel might be an example. When she's not working at the museum, doing construction jobs at her house, or entertaining friends with David, Rachel devotes her time to playing tennis and rarely captures a moment to focus on other issues in her life, like when to start a family.

If you're more family oriented, as June is, you might ignore the career or the social side of life. And we all know highly charged professionals, like Betty, who have put their careers before everything else, including their health. That's one of the main reasons why

Betty came to the Ranch: Her weight was beginning to balloon, and her spirit was suffering from the stress she had imposed on herself by working day and night.

We all tend to focus on certain parts of the Wheel and ignore others. But when we do, all aspects of our lives eventually suffer. If your finances are troubled, then odds are at some point your health, your social life, your family relationships, your work, and yes, even your sex life will suffer.

Is your life out of balance? If it is, you probably know or suspect it. Check in with whatever part of your body senses your overall well-being. For me it's my stomach. I get a bad feeling right in the middle when I need to take some action about a situation that could endanger my future or violate my sense of right and wrong—and I'm not doing anything about it. That terrible feeling lets me know that my life is out of kilter; it's a call for me to get into gear. For you, the signal might be a backache, an awful rash, or a piercing migraine, like the ones that cripple Maggie. Pay attention to those feelings; they're telling you that things aren't working so smoothly, and that it's time to take some action.

CASH FOR YOUR FINANCIAL FUTURE!

When I mentioned to the women at the Ranch the bad feeling I get in my stomach when my life is out of balance, Linette understood right away. "That's the feeling I've been having lately," she said. "It's like the bottom has fallen out of my stomach. And I know it's because of the divorce and my husband's affair. But it's also because of my fear that I had been left out of the loop in my marriage, as far as money goes."

A waiter delivered our entrées, an eggplant lasagna and a medley of zucchini, cauliflower, and string beans, as we continued talking over dinner.

"I'm sure none of us wants to be financially upset, with that gnawing, unpleasant feeling roiling in the pit of our stomachs—especially when we're having such delicious food and doing other good things for ourselves," I said.

"You got that right," Betty said with a laugh, savoring the lasagna. "But seriously, I pretty much know what I want for my financial future."

"I do, too," added Rachel.

June stared, a quizzical look on her face. "You know," she mused, "that's something I've never really thought about."

"Why not?" Sadie asked.

"I guess because I don't think it applies to me. I feel very secure about how my husband takes care of me," June answered curtly.

"What if you didn't have a husband?" Linette challenged. "Then what would you want?"

June was silent for a beat before answering, "I don't know."

"I think what we all want is very simple," I said. "I don't think many of us set out to be extremely rich. Rather, what we truly want is a good 'feeling' about money and our future—a feeling of financial security and well-being. We want to know that we're going to be okay in all seven areas of our Wheel of Life. Our hopes and dreams include all seven spokes: good health, caring relationships, a secure and fulfilling job, meaningful friendships, mental and spiritual growth—and no financial problems."

"What do *you* want out of life, Joan?" Maggie inquired.

"First, I want to be secure. Then, I want to build wealth to the maximum of my talents, because then I can follow Oprah's lead and give some away to make the world a better place," I said. "But the first stage is definitely personal security—knowing that my needs and the needs of my family will be reasonably well met even if I'm not working."

"Hey, I hear you," Linette interjected. "After the marriage I was in, I definitely want to be financially independent. And I don't ever want to have an emergency I can't handle. But the most important consideration for me is my daughter's education."

"How about you, Betty?" I asked.

"Well, I feel lucky," she responded. "I've made good money, so

I've been able to buy most of the things I want. As for my future . . . well, I just want to make sure that I can live comfortably, on my own—following my passions—and that I won't have to depend on family or friends—"

"Or shrinking government programs," I suggested.

"Right. And you know something else? Like you—and Oprah— I'd also like to make a contribution and give something back to society," Betty continued.

"I feel very strongly about that, too," Sadie said. "I've been working with inner-city kids in Boston, teaching them how to read and write. It's an after-school program, and the youngsters are such a joy. I'm so proud of them, and I get such good psychic rewards from the work. I took my group to a bookstore in Harvard Square one day and told them they could each pick out a book to read and I'd buy it for them, but only on the condition that they tell me all about the book when they're done."

"That's way cool," Maggie said. "So do you have any book reports yet?"

"Yes and no. They haven't finished reading, but they're giving me chapter-by-chapter recitals." Sadie laughed. "At least they're reading. Some of the kids could never do that before."

The futures my friends envisioned grow from very human desires. Their dreams are practicalities rather than luxuries, lives of sharing and caring. Wouldn't you be happy if you could fulfill them? I know I would, even though I have more than modest desires. But these are goals that lead to rich, fulfilling lives, and they are obtainable for all women.

We finished dinner and parted for the rest of the evening. I made a mental note to speak privately with Linette and Maggie. Both seemed to need a friend, someone to listen. Betty's enthusiasm about tackling her finances clearly had been sparked, and she asked to see me professionally when we both got home. Rachel and Sadie had the same interest. Only June was reluctant to think more about her money life. Still, I suspected that our chat had awakened some concerns of hers that had been dormant.

Two days later, I spoke at the Ranch about money and its role in our lives as women. The room overflowed with women of all ages from many walks of life.

I began by talking to this friendly gathering about my own relationship with money.

2

Financial Jewels:
The Truth About Money

Love and Money
Women's Financial Revolution
Snapping the Spending Chain
A Wake-up Call
Beginning Today
Financial Jewels

*T*began: "Ever since I was a child, I had a taste for nice things. And when I grew older, I learned to love beautiful clothes, excellent shoes, good leather handbags, and well-designed jewelry. But I certainly didn't know how I would be able to afford everything I desired, nor did my parents. In fact, shortly before I graduated from college, I recall my father telling me, 'Joan, you're not going to be able to live on minimum wage.' Boy, was he right! And it didn't take too long for me to encounter my first money crisis, which surfaced when I decided to go to graduate school.

"My parents paid my tuition for college—Denison University in Granville, Ohio—where, thinking I would go to nursing school, I majored in biology. But the brewing feminist storm of the 1970s helped pilot me in another direction—business school. Without knowing exactly what the business world would be like, I sensed I'd have a lot more freedom and opportunity and different challenges than I would as a nurse. Today, it's fairly common for women to seek an MBA. But in 1974, business school was a new frontier for females. And for graduate school, I was financially on my own.

"My pioneer days began in Nashville, Tennessee, at the Owen Graduate School of Management at Vanderbilt University, and that's where my first money challenges began. My tuition, room, and board for the year came to about $10,000. I had borrowed part of the money for my grad school costs from the government's student loan program, and I had received partial scholarships from Betty Crocker and Oscar Mayer. But the rest of the money eluded me. I lay awake at nights wondering how I was ever going to pay the school, and needless to say, I had one giant stomachache.

"I worked long and hard to keep afloat. I held three jobs. I was a clerk in the dean's office and an assistant in the school library. I also worked as an aide to the state treasurer in Tennessee reviewing state programs, like minimum-security prisons and group homes for troubled adolescents. But what I earned still wasn't always enough to keep me going. I was very much alone. I felt insecure and frightened, and I remember thinking how nice it would be to have a trust fund—something that would regularly pay me cash without my having to work so hard for it.

"My money tensions threw my Wheel of Life into a skid. I didn't eat properly and began losing weight. Emotionally, I became extremely uptight about practically everything and allowed little things to upset my peace of mind. I felt like I was struggling to survive—and I was. But my anxieties did not defeat me. In retrospect, although I considered myself poor when I was in grad school, I was really poor only in my thinking. And with poverty on the brain, I made some unfortunate choices. A few had long-term complications."

LOVE AND MONEY

"To begin with, I borrowed $2,500 from the guy I was dating so I could finish grad school and earn my MBA. It seemed like all the money in the world to me, and in my desperation to complete my degree, I allowed love and money to get hopelessly entangled. I wound up marrying this man, and in my heart of hearts I knew that one of the reasons I was marrying him was because I was afraid I couldn't pay back my loan. That may seem silly now, but not too many women—even a woman with an MBA—were secure about their own abilities in 1975, despite the flowering of the women's movement.

"Then I compounded the error by taking a wrong turn in my career, again allowing love and money to become entangled. I turned down the job I really wanted: financial analyst in the commercial credit department of a bank in the South. Instead, I accepted the same position for less money at a bank in the same state because my husband-to-be was working in the same city.

"Looking back, I now find it interesting that I never really considered the universe of available jobs. I could have worked anywhere in the world, and the opportunities probably would have been far greater in any of a dozen cities around the country, but I didn't have the courage to seek out those jobs because I felt bound to go where my fiancé was. This was a strange time for women because it was well before many of the molds in which we were formed were still unbroken. And one of the assumptions I hadn't shaken was that a woman "followed her man." Negotiating a fair, equal compromise between partners wasn't an option.

"We didn't get married immediately. Instead, I began to carve out a career for myself in banking. I was earning about $25,000 a year. At the time, it was one of the highest salaries that particular bank had ever paid a woman. Unfortunately, business school didn't teach me very much about personal finances, so I squeezed my paycheck to buy clothes, trinkets, and items for my apartment.

"Grad school had also neglected to teach me other lessons, too—lessons my first job taught me about the place of women in corporate America. Welcome to the world of sexual harassment and the glass ceiling—the world of corporate America—where the playing field is built on male language and male rules. All of these, I discovered, can play havoc with a woman's sense of well-being and financial security."

Sexual Harassment and a Woman's Sense of Financial Security

At this point in my speech at the Ranch, I could tell that the women in the audience understood my message all too well. As my eyes darted about the room, I saw a sea of bobbing heads. And their faces told me that the story I went on to tell sparked some similar memories.

"The bank I worked for ran a credit school, where we learned all about lending, and I was the only woman in the class. At the end of the course, the participants celebrated with a party. I was sitting at a table with a group of other students when a top officer of the bank—let's call him Jack—sat down next to me. At first, I was pleased to be noticed. But then I was stunned when, after some small talk, he leaned closer and whispered, 'So, you live alone. Why don't I come back and spend the night with you?'

"I was dumbfounded. It was immediately obvious to me that my job, which I badly needed, was at stake. But so were my integrity and self-esteem. I quickly scanned my mind for a response and asked, 'Wouldn't your wife miss you?'

" 'No,' Jack replied. Besides, he boasted, he kept a change of clothes in his office.

"Finally, with as much boldness as I could muster, I turned to him and said, 'Listen, Jack. The first thing you learn in business school is not to sleep your way up the ladder!'

"He smirked and replied, 'Joan, this is not "up the ladder." This is the top!' Chagrined, confused, and humiliated, I awkwardly excused myself and left the party.

"I now know that, whether I had succumbed to his wishes or not, I would have lost either way. Within a few weeks, it was clear I was finished at that job. One day, I walked as usual onto the 'national lending platform'—the area of the bank where all the loan officers sat—only to hear another lending officer broadcast to the rest of the room, while brandishing a book in his hand, 'This is the story of Joan's sex life—and all the pages are blank!'

"It was clear that word had gotten around that I had turned down a proposition from Jack. Suddenly, my coworkers were acting coldly toward me. Hoping I would fail, lending officers began heaping more and more work on me.

"A woman who's been there understands the stress, confusion, humilation, and fear you suffer day in and day out when victimized by sexual harassment. I found it hard to continue working, but hung in there while continuing to ask myself if it was worth it. I know many women who have asked themselves the same question under similar circumstances. It was a relief when my fiancé was transferred, because it gave me an easy excuse to resign.

"So I got married and moved with my husband to Philadelphia, where I spent most of the 1980s working with Wall Street investment firms. While I hung in there to gain professional knowledge, they were years filled with similar situations of harassment, power games, and low blows.

"How does harassment figure in a discussion of women and money? In our society, women have to stomach a lot in order to move up the professional ladder and progress in a career. I went through what many women at the time endured. Sadly, not all survived. Thank goodness Anita Hill opened up this discussion for all of us.

"But today's generation of women needs to gain something of value from the challenging path they've plowed through. Having struggled to breach the corporate wall and survive the harassment minefield, we need to walk away with more than just scars. Certainly, we need a renewed sense of dignity and pride in our status as females in an often hostile world. But we also need cash. If we reach our later years and have little money to show for our efforts, then we will have lost—big time."

WOMEN'S FINANCIAL REVOLUTION

"This is a time for women to go beyond bill paying and to plan for *their* financial future. Now, this is heady stuff—a revolution—because having such financial responsibility and power is brand new for many of us, something that didn't exist a decade or two ago. But it is also one more step in the march toward freedom and the realization of our power as women. But unless women take steps to create their financial freedom, everything we've fought for, everything we've achieved professionally, socially, politically, and philosophically will be wasted."

A hand shot up in the audience. "How are we to realize this freedom?" a woman asked.

"The answer is that we have to rethink a few things that have held us back," I replied. "To begin with, many of us continue to link up some very weird concepts concerning money. The most prevalent, I think, is confusing love and money. This often causes us to give other people responsibility for our financial lives, preventing us from ever learning how to have control of our own futures.

"Like many women, I once united love and money, although because of my basic insecurity, it took years before I realized it.

"It began in childhood. My parents were never very demonstrative in showing love—back then, we weren't the type to hug and kiss a lot. But when they gave me my allowance, I always felt happy. I concluded that receiving money was a strong communication of love.

"It followed that if I was denied money, it meant that I wasn't loved. Once when I was in college, at Denison University, I asked my father to put some money into my checking account for sorority expenses. When he refused, I felt it meant that he didn't like me anymore. Of course, that was not the case. He just thought that I had spent enough money that semester. But my reaction was an emotional, not a logical, one.

"I'm not alone in falsely linking love and money. Nor am I the only woman who ever mixed up emotional insecurities with financial insecurities. But the problem was a consistent one for many years in my life. Looking back on my first marriage, I see how money became a lightning rod for emotional and psychological problems. Because my husband and I couldn't talk about other issues, we always fought about money. According to a plan he devised, we were supposed to split all our bills. This wasn't quite how it worked out, however. I earned about the same amount of money as he did in his marketing job for a steel company, but I gave up more than half my paycheck to the household expenses.

"Furthermore, like many women at that time, I also allowed my husband to take charge of paying the bills and making all our investments. Our money fights contributed significantly to my decision to end the marriage. By the time I left him, I had no idea what investments and cash we had or even how to access them"—the same bind in which Linette, the soon-to-be-divorced marketing specialist, now finds herself. "The truth is that when I left him, I became destitute—I felt what it was like to be on the streets and to wonder how my basic needs were going to be met. How could this happen to me—an MBA? My husband had controlled all the assets and I had nothing. Since I had left him so quickly, he was angry, and at that point, he wasn't going to give me anything. The lawyers dragged their feet and wanted me to pay them before they made things happen. It wasn't a pretty picture. Eventually, I had to depend on my family. Luckily, they were there.

"It's ironic. Here I was, someone who worked in the investment world, and I was as dumb as a mongoose regarding my own money concerns. I still longed for a trust fund, but at no time had I stopped to ask myself, 'What am I doing to make sure I don't become a bag lady? What am I doing to ensure my financial future?' I had surrendered control of my finances in the name of love, and now I had no game plan of my own. And I knew that my money confusion was limiting my options and preventing me from getting on with life.

"It's interesting how love slows down the brain when it comes to money. I've had unmarried female clients tell me that, in their heart of hearts, they believed that if they had their financial futures all set up and were independent, they'd never attract a man. *'How can a man care for me, if I can take care of myself?'*—their brains queried. It's a peculiar slant in our culture: A man doesn't want, or is threatened by, a woman who assumes what society traditionally has considered to be a man's role—providing and controlling the cash. The corollary is that if you accumulate money before the love of your life comes along, you might make yourself less lovable. A woman might shy away from being more savvy about money than the man in her life so she won't appear to be ahead of him in the money game. 'Women aren't supposed to do better than a man,' we've been wrongly told.

"Where do all these weird ideas come from? And why do they persist after decades of battles on behalf of the rights and freedoms of women? Who knows. Whatever the source, all of this antiquated thinking limits our sense of self and keeps us dependent. By confusing love and money, we put off making long-term financial plans. And without these plans, our futures will always be in doubt."

SNAPPING THE SPENDING CHAIN

"You can't feel healthy and competent in all areas of your Wheel of Life, you can't look forward to a stable tomorrow, and you can't feel you're doing right by yourself and your family unless you make your money work for you.

"If you're spending your money as fast as you earn it, it's not working for you. If your money is sitting in a checking account doing nothing, it's not working for you. If you've made no investments for your future, your money's not working for you. And if you have investments but don't know what they are or how they're doing, your money's not working for you."

I surveyed the audience and saw some knowing smiles. "You, too, huh?" I said.

"For many years, I failed to make my money work for me. Instead, what money I earned poured through my hands like water.

"This has been painfully true for many working women, who find themselves spending money on clothes, accessories, and grooming because they must always look good. There are also the added maintenance costs—cleaning, laundry, and salon bills—to keep clothes, hair, and nails looking good, and this maintenance can slice a big chunk from a paycheck.

"And women spend their money on other things as well, like vacations, cars, and entertainment. Some drop bundles on furniture, high-tech kitchen appliances and sports equipment, or overpriced health clubs and personal trainers. Many others fix up their homes or spend their money on their children, husbands, or partners. And then there are those women who have no idea how the money spills from their wallets—it simply disappears by the end of the week, and they feel anxious and guilty that the cash is gone.

"There are lots of good things about spending and enjoying your money. But when this comes before investing for your future, that's when your Wheel's out of balance. Once you've developed strategies to create your financial future, you'll be able to spend money guilt free and find true joy.

"My curiosity about money led to some new insights. When I went to work in Philadelphia for an investment banking firm, I thought that I would be in a position to learn about and master the mysteries of money. I had the notion that I would be in a place where I would be initiated into the world of finance and taught how to build wealth. I certainly had the opportunity to hear all the experts—the big guns in the industry—chatter about investment selection, business and industry trends, and the future of the U.S. economy. But after working and listening for a few months, I began to wonder: 'Am I the only one who went to this movie and didn't get the ending? I'm not building personal wealth; instead, I'm spending everything I earn. What am I doing? When do I start to benefit from the supposed wisdom of the financial experts?'

"Soon I discovered that I wasn't alone in the way I was living. Looking around, I saw many other people whose lives were a precarious financial balancing act. Many of these same people were giving investment advice to our firm's clients! Something was truly out of whack.

"Financially, I had not yet learned to trust myself, but I was also wise enough not to believe everything Wall Street had told me about investing. It's a funny thing: I was an investment banker responsible for structuring municipal bond packages for $20 and $30 million; I had a reputation for being innovative and particularly good at making the deal. But I was clueless about making consistently good investments for myself. I did make a few investments. I even purchased some valuable stocks, like IBM. But I didn't think of keeping my stock for the long haul. Instead, I later sold my shares and used the money for living expenses. This stock could have been the starting point for a long-term investment plan, but at the time, I wasn't allowing my investments to grow. I was wallowing in financial insecurity.

"I see now that I was focusing on acting the role rather than using what I had learned in my professional life to benefit my personal life. The strategies I was practicing then were focused on how I could spend money to look the part of the well-appointed investment banker, so maybe I would look more competent—a short-term solution."

A WAKE-UP CALL

"I began to think more about the importance of having a fund of money for my future after my marriage ended—a time when I saw the reality of basic needs with great clarity.

"The divorce didn't generate a nest egg for me. What hadn't been spent, my husband kept for himself. When I left him, I walked away with little more than my car, the clothes on my back, and my American Express card. I felt the discomfort of being without a backup, and my old dream of a trust fund came back to me with a vivid intensity. The pain of being alone and financially adrift was acute. Often, I imagined the worst. Slowly I realized that it was up to me to create my own 'trust fund.' In the years following my divorce, I set out to learn strategies that would put me on a course to have more control over my financial future."

As I spoke that sentence, I scanned the speakers' room at the Ranch until my eyes locked on Linette. From the little she had told me, I knew she was experiencing what I had. I went back to my speech, but not before I caught a glimpse of her quietly slipping out the door. I made a mental note to seek her out the next day. I continued my talk.

"After patching up the wounds from my divorce, I went back to work. By using ingenuity, creativity, and determination forged by my experience, I prepared myself to look for new financial opportunities from the cash flow of working. One of my first successful plans grew out of an opportunity arising from my work. The time was right: a large block of municipal bonds was available for a lot less than their full price. The bonds could pay me $20,000 a year in tax-free interest for as long as I owned them. At the time (the early 1980s), that would have been enough not only to pay my rent but also to pay at least minimal expenses. This was pretty close to the trust fund for security I'd imagined!

"I was in a very lucky position. Municipal bonds were something I knew about because of the work I had been doing. The bonds I purchased at that time were from a project about to go bankrupt— a life-care facility for the elderly—but I believed it could recover from its problems. If I was right, the bonds would become more valuable as the facility did. So I took some bonus money and also margined the bonds by paying 50 percent of the cost and borrowing the rest, and made the investment. It was a big leap for me. I remember thinking, 'There's enough income from these bonds so I could eke out a living even if I didn't have another source.' At least it would be enough to cover the essentials for my dignity—to meet my basic needs. It was a stretch and a step to building personal security.

"But at the same time, I was becoming increasingly insecure about being able to continue making money in the investment banking industry because of the constant challenges of the workplace. Discrimination in the business was rampant, and it seemed that someone was always trying to jack up the stakes and set up us women to fail. Some of us did; many more survived. But at what cost to our health, our spirits, and our relationships?

"Under the circumstances, I never really knew if there would be a tomorrow. I felt that roiling sensation in my stomach, and I knew something was out of balance. There definitely was a big discrepancy between the size of the nest egg I'd established and the way I really wanted to live. I intuitively knew that if something interfered with my income, life would be very different . . . and not necessarily good.

"My world took a tumble around 1984."

Creating My Own Corporate Culture

"I was working at an investment banking firm, sitting in a large room filled with wall-to-wall men—I was the only professional woman. Each morning, I filled a beautiful glass bowl I kept on my desk with a glowing display of yellow tulips. It was a symbolic gesture, of course; I was determined to be feminine but tough in the work world. Apparently, however, I was the only one enjoying the tulips' explosion of color. The men told me the flowers 'disrupted' their work environment; they were a distraction and just didn't 'fit in' with the rest of the room.

"But the beauty of the yellow tulips encouraged me, and I continued to work at a productive clip. I sold a large block of municipal bonds to a client who was head of surgery at a Philadelphia hospital. I received the usual slip of paper from my firm confirming that I had indeed sold the bonds to that particular client. But about three weeks later, the firm informed me that the bonds could not be delivered to my customer, because they were 'never available.' I was furious, of course, and convinced that one of the other traders had snatched the bonds for one of his clients—traders sometimes pull such dirty deeds. But I was also determined to have the firm live up to its commitment to my client. I insisted that he be given a similar investment—another package of bonds at the same price.

"Several days later, the office manager called me on the carpet. 'You don't seem to be playing on the firm's team,' he complained. This confused me, because I thought that serving my client would be in the best interest of my 'team.' But the firm thought differently. They hated me for standing up to them, just as they hated the tulips.

"The truth is, had I been male, the same thing might have happened to me, because this is how the brokerage business operates. But I had to stand up for my client and for my values, and I simply had to create an environment in which I could live: The tulips were going to stay. Suddenly, I found myself starting my own business so that I could create a more livable work environment for myself— one with a corporate culture that reflected my personality and beliefs. Oh, I could have gone to work for another firm, but I sensed that the same problems would dog me, because that certainly had been the pattern for me and for many other women then and even now. I wasn't the only woman who could not live a full life on Wall Street. But going the distance wasn't the issue. Quite simply, I no longer wanted to live in the harshness of a work world I didn't manage; I no longer wanted to have other people chart and control my destiny.

"Leaving the security of a corporate job wasn't easy for me; it took all my courage to become an independent businesswoman with my own name on the door. But I took the plunge. I started the first female-owned investment banking firm in the United States to underwrite and distribute municipal bonds—that is, debt certificates issued by state and local governments to finance buildings and other projects in various communities.

"Fortunately, I had already built up a network of contacts among municipal finance managers, and I was able to use it to launch my new business. I went to the city treasurer in Philadelphia and requested that my company be allowed to be an underwriter for bonds issued by the city. My company helped underwrite a municipal bond issue for the Philadelphia school board. As a result, we became the first female-owned investment banking firm to underwrite a municipal bond issue in the United States.

"In time, Perry Investments Inc. was the investment banker for many major municipal projects. We helped underwrite the financing for such projects as the United Airlines terminal at O'Hare International Airport and the new Comiskey Park in Chicago, and the parking complex at the Philadelphia International Airport. We also handled a part of the bond refinancing of the Moscone Center in San Francisco, and helped several state governments, including that of California, to put together bond issues. My firm owned large blocks of municipal bonds—tens of millions of dollars' worth—and sold the bonds to bond funds and institutional investors—pension funds, college endowments, and the like.

"I loved this work and I was good at it. Running Perry Investments gave me the opportunity to broadcast to the world that women could take on a challenging financial job and its risks and rewards. Soon my firm was visible enough to influence perceptions about women on Wall Street, which helped me to expand the opportunities for women in the big male-dominated brokerage firms. I got a not-so-small thrill from knowing that the firm I'd left was seeing Perry Investments' name on bonds they were trying to obtain.

"I did little things to help keep our firm and its special status in the industry visible. For example, when I started my firm, I chose pink stationery. Everyone warned me not to use pink in the navy blue, pin-striped investment world. But my mother, who had created a successful travel business, always said, 'You don't have to worry about what people say about you. It's only when you are unimportant enough *not* to be talked about that you have to worry.' I embraced my mother's philosophy, and stuck with pink.

"Being unusual had its advantages. One day, I was in the state treasurer's office, and I asked him if he had received our bond proposal. He pointed to a huge stack of proposals in the corner of his office and said, 'Oh, yes. How could I miss it? Yours is the pink one in the middle there.' "

Investment Mistakes

"Meanwhile, despite the success of my business, my personal financial education was proceeding slowly. Here I was, thirty-six years old, with $100,000 simmering in my business checking account and naive about how to employ it. I had made that cash, and I did not want to allow it to just sit and gather dust. I was grateful for how far I had come professionally, and although I recognized the need to generate more money, I was also cautious about Wall Street because of my experience as an investment banker. As a consequence, I turned away from the stock market and began to experiment in other investment areas.

"Perhaps you feel uneasy because you know little about putting your money to work. I've made my share of zany money choices, as you'll see. But I've also learned from these sometimes painful experiences, and I eventually carved out some effective strategies for myself.

"My first investment outside of the stock and bond markets was—believe it or not—in a friend's egg roll company. He was an older man who, in my estimation, had been extremely successful in business. He had built a hotel in China and had other projects that seemed to be financially sound, and they had made him a millionaire many times over. Besides, he was a friend, and I thought he would also take care of my money. I gave him $50,000 for a piece of Eggroll Fantasy, a company that produces the highest-quality egg rolls on the market. The company makes eight different varieties, including chicken cashew, broccoli and cheese, shrimp, vegetarian, and beef teriyaki. The egg rolls are sold wholesale to restaurants and hotels, and served at Madison Square Garden in New York City and even at the White House. It all sounded great.

"But the real story was that things inside the company weren't working well. I discovered that the business had a host of problems: overspending, flat sales growth, and serious management weaknesses. To help right the company and protect my investment, I became a member of the board of directors. And one of the corrective steps we had to take was to insist on my friend's resignation from the firm's management. So far, the only benefit I've derived from my $50,000 is that I get to eat egg rolls whenever I want to."

This story gets a laugh whenever I tell it, and the audience at the Ranch was no exception. I laughed, too, because I no longer feel the sting of this unfortunate investment choice. Besides, the egg rolls are delicious.

"I must admit, though, that if my investment education had to be based on learning from mistakes, I've been thorough about it! My next misguided investment choice involved a medical supply company. The company made ceramic sterilizers. The technology was superb, but the management was inept. I lost another $15,000.

"Even with my MBA, I made these mistakes and simply didn't get it. I trusted others instead of myself and, more important strategically, I didn't trust the stock market. If I had just put my money into two good mutual funds, whose managers were making sound investments in the stock market, this money would have more than tripled in value today.

"These blunders could have been critical. I took part of my security money—money I needed for my future—and blew it. I was gambling my future with my heart and soul, not to mention my butt, which surely would be sitting on the street.

"One night, as I thrashed about in bed desperately trying to sleep, the folly of my misadventures in investing slammed into me. I sat bolt upright from under the covers and said to myself: 'You've got to get it together, honey!' I realized that even though I had worked in investment houses, handling billions of dollars, and even though my own business was now generating a respectable income, I had no plan to ensure *my* future well-being and comfort. If I wasn't careful, I could make it big real fast and lose it in a blink.

"All of this might sound painfully familiar to you—you may have your own investment horror stories to tell, whether it was $100, $1,000, $100,000, or $1 million that got scooped from your hands. I know one woman—she is in her early thirties—who finally escaped the dungeons of credit card despair and managed to accumulate $3,500 in a money market account. She planned to drop it into a mutual fund, but a friend told her to invest the money instead in a hot new company that sold 'cutting-edge' beauty-care products. She could have a piece of the company, sell the products, and triple her money within a month. The young woman followed her friend's advice and lost her entire $3,500 in a pyramid scheme—an elaborate scam in which only a handful of people at the top actually make money, while everyone else is left trying to sell expensive soap and shampoo to their friends and neighbors.

"Let's not judge our mistakes too harshly. Let's not cry over setbacks or let them stop us from future investing. What's important is that we learn from our journeys and adopt new attitudes that will take us down some different paths in the future. Above all, we have to reject the idea of quick cash and instant riches and, instead, welcome the principle of *lasting cash*."

Setting Strategies

"Before crafting a plan, I needed some ammunition so I'd know what to do. I began to read everything I could get my hands on— money books, investment publications. I went to as many financial seminars by critical thinkers as I could. And I started to do some really deep thinking about the situations I'd seen during my career on Wall Street. I studied what worked and what didn't.

"When I'm curious, I also take surveys. So I turned to women I knew and began to ask one question"—a question I put to the audience at the Ranch and one I will put to you right now: " 'What are you doing now to make sure you'll have financial well-being for your life when you ease out of working?'

"The first time I posed my question, it happened spontaneously as I took a long stroll in the park with my friend Nora. Nora usually didn't have time for walks because she is so dedicated to her work as a lawyer. On that day, I turned to her and said, 'You know, we've both made a lot more money than we ever expected when we planned our careers. But where are we going to be when we're sixty years old? What are you doing to make sure you don't end up a bag lady?'

"My friend's eyes widened at the mention of 'bag lady,' and I knew that I'd struck a chord. She turned to me and said, 'Well, I have a car and a house, and that's about where I am right now.'

"A few days later, I talked to another dear friend, Sylvia. She gave me the same answer: She had a car and a house. A pattern was emerging. I pressed on.

"That night, I called a woman I had known in college. We often chatted by phone just to stay in touch, but rarely saw each other. She lived in New York City, was married with two children, and did a little freelance editing when she had the time. I asked her the same question. 'We own a co-op here in the city,' she replied. 'What about a car?' I asked. 'Are you kidding? No. I take the kids around on the bus or the subway,' she said. Whew! No car.

"I even talked to the woman who cuts my hair. Guess what? She owns a small two-bedroom house and, yes, a car.

"Finally, I decided to go straight to the source. I called my friend Jackie, an investment banker at Merrill Lynch. Surely, I figured, she would have some brilliant inside strategies for her personal finances. We arranged to meet for lunch one day, and after our entrées had been served, I turned the talk to money matters.

" 'So I guess Merrill Lynch has an excellent investment program for employees. You're so busy traveling from city to city, there's someone at Merrill whose only job is to make sure that your earnings are well invested, right?' I asked. I envisioned a committee that provides the company's investment expertise to employees to ensure that they will have financial peace of mind so they can then do their jobs better.

"I almost dropped my fork at Jackie's response. 'Well, the fact is,' she said, 'I invested in some Merrill funds and lost money, so instead, I just bought a big house. Oh yes, I have a BMW and a Range Rover, too.'

"The pattern was clear. My baby-boomer friends were 'investing' in houses and cars and then stopping because they, too, hadn't come up with any good strategies for growing their money. Our parents, our schools, our employers, our financial institutions, our popular culture—not one had taught my friends and me how to use our money.

"Something was seriously wrong.

"Where we are today regarding money matters is very much where we were a decade ago regarding personal fitness. At one time it was commonly believed that if you ran at full speed, jumped up and down a lot, and sweated profusely, then you would eventually become physically fit and thin. Today the more accepted wisdom is that old-fashioned anaerobic exercise—the kind in which you're moving so hard that you can't talk—actually sends your body into survival mode. As a result, the body stores fat, probably defeating any weight-loss or health goals you seek through exercise. Now we know that a regular walk in the park that involves both your body and spirit will produce consistent physical and mental benefits.

"And we can find other examples of common beliefs that are now outmoded: for example, our past beliefs about nutrition. When I was growing up, we were told to eat three large, balanced meals a day in order to be healthy and fit. Today, many nutritionists and doctors say that four or five smaller, low-fat meals—one or two of them being fresh fruit or vegetables—make a more healthful diet.

"Thankfully, the word about proper exercise and diet is spreading rapidly among women of all ages. But many women are still in the dark about money matters. And Wall Street itself deserves much of the blame.

"At many of the major Wall Street brokerage houses I knew, the primary approach to building wealth was to make big chunks of money for the client—and, more important, for the broker—all at once. No value was placed on slowly, patiently building a bundle for the future. If you buy into that living-for-the-moment rush, then yes, the risks are very high, and the anxieties of first-time investors are an understandable reaction to the frenzied Wall Street approach. But beneath the hype and excitement of the 'fast money' game is the real motive for the financial industry: generating the highest possible commissions for unscrupulous brokers and increasing the wealth of the firm.

"When I worked on Wall Street, I noticed that the investment information itself wasn't too tough to understand, but it was often presented in a jumbled manner that was heavy on jargon and short on simplicity and logic. It almost seemed that someone deliberately wanted to make financial information confusing to the average consumer. I noticed also that brokerage statements presented information in ways that confused clients and often omitted essential information—like what a client paid for a specific investment and its current value. With a little effort to straighten it all out, though, and to put it into sensible language, nothing was particularly difficult.

"Eventually, I realized that the financial community is interested more in separating you from your money than in building your wealth. As a result, investor education is a low priority. Even those of us who worked on Wall Street making your investments were never really taught how to handle our own personal finances, or to lead others to grow wealth."

"You mean you knew how to invest other people's money but not your own?" someone in the audience asked.

"No. It wasn't that. The point is that Wall Street isn't really interested in investing your money, only in getting you to spend it," I replied. "Let me explain.

"Wall Street teaches the investor to 'buy in greed and sell in fear.' What does that mean? I'll give you an example: Your broker calls to give you the following hot tip: 'FLASH—XYZ stock is really HOT.

It's about to go through the roof. You should buy it.' Well, if you have a few bucks sitting in your checking account, you may well say okay and take the plunge.

"Several weeks later, the price of the stock has declined and you begin to get nervous. What happened to that great opportunity? Your broker's answers are confusing, even evasive. And the business page of your local paper runs a story about how XYZ company's profits are way below expectations. Naturally, you think, 'I really wouldn't want to lose all of my money.' So you opt to sell the stock.

"Bottom line—you bought in greed and sold in fear. The only person who benefited was the broker, who made commissions on both the buy and the sell.

"I once bought a stock called Bolt Technologies in the way I just described, and that burning sensation in my stomach clearly indicated that I'd made a mistake. I wound up selling it at a loss. Because of this unfortunate experience, I was discouraged from investing in stocks again for a long time.

"The right wealth-building strategy is just the opposite from what some on Wall Street practice. Rather than buying today's 'hot' investment, you want to buy something that other people disregard and keep it until others value it. In this way, you'll 'buy low and sell high'—the dream of every ambitious investor. As this book will show you, this strategy is the only reliable way to grow your money for a secure financial future.

"Furthermore, now's the time to develop and rely upon your own judgment when it comes to making your dollars work for you. Decades ago, many women went to male doctors, who often didn't listen to what a woman had to say about her own body, but who presumed to know all the answers himself. This happens to women and their money, too—a woman's competence is questioned and she's treated like a baby. For women, the path to building wealth is using self-knowledge, making more personal decisions, and preserving their power to choose their own direction. With this in place, then perhaps you'll partner with someone else who can increase your knowledge. There are plenty of Wall Street brokers, financial advisers, and get-rich-quick scam artists who would be happy to help you gamble away your bucks. The wealth-building strategy is to keep clear of them and to chart your course. And don't be put off investing by a few bad-boy—and bad-girl—brokers. Believe me, the stock market is a proven wealth builder when you use the right approach.

BEGINNING TODAY

"Sooner or later nearly all women, because of divorce or other lifestyle changes, come nose-to-nose with the financial area of their lives. You won't want to learn how to handle money matters in a crisis; it's better to learn while you can be patient and reflective.

"But so many women confront their cash concerns only at the worst moments in their lives—when they divorce, when their husbands die, when they lose their jobs, or when they face a health crisis.

"So when is a good time to start caring for your financial future? Today!

"It doesn't take a course in economics to see that the longer you wait, the worse off you may be. The facts aren't always easy to face, but they are potent persuaders. They show the need to create a sound base for your future financial life now, whether you're married, single, widowed, divorced, or partnered. All women, working and nonworking, need to provide for the years when their earning power has diminished or ended altogether. They'll need cash—just as Sophie Tucker said.

"We all know this to be true, or we should, because we live in a time of extended longevity. According to the U.S. Department of Health and Human Services, a fifty-five-year-old woman today has about 26.2 years left to live. Thus, she can anticipate living to the age of eighty-one. A man's life expectancy is a few years shorter—seventy-five. And the truth is that with good health, you can live well into your nineties.

"Most women can expect to be on their own at some point in

their lives. Many, of course, remain single. Others, by either choice or circumstance, become single. At least half of all first marriages in the United States end in divorce or separation, and so do more than half of all second marriages. Many women base their lifestyles on a two-income household, and women who work at home as mothers and homemakers choose to depend on their husbands or partners for financial support. Our longevity means that most of us will be living for a long time. So divorce and other circumstances are likely to leave many women in charge of their financial lives, regardless of income, whether they're ready or not.

"Many men are fine providers for their wives and children and carefully plan for the time when their spouses—whether working or nonworking—will be on their own. Others, however, are less responsible, through either ignorance, carelessness, or unwillingness to face the harsh realities of life. In too many cases, this means that these men are leaving their wives and children to slide into poverty after they die.

"If you've digested all this, then your stomach may be burning by now. Every single one of these contingencies is a serious challenge to gastrointestinal equilibrium.

"And these realities shed a very different light on the belief many women have that investing is risky business. If you take these considerations very seriously, then you'll realize that spending your money as you earn it, without putting it to work, is the real risk you face, and it's a far greater risk than the chance that you'll lose money by having an agreement with yourself to regularly invest your money in a way that nurtures and benefits you. The real risk most women face is *failing* to invest actively.

"And part of this life process is being patient and trusting the reality that your money needs time to grow. This is a reality that's not going to sprout overnight, like a Chia Pet. It's going to grow based on consistent investment action, not one based on hot tips, inside information, advice from a psychic hot line, or terrifying chance-taking that will only send your stomach into hyperspace. Believe it or not, your money can grow without financial worry."

This was the substance of my talk to the women at the Ranch. By the time I finished, many of the women were alive with new energy—ready to consider different opportunities for themselves.

FINANCIAL JEWELS

A few weeks after I returned to my office, Betty Scott, the lawyer from San Francisco, called. She was ready to find out more about how to grow her money. I'm going to give you some jewels—financial jewels—in this book and, through Betty, you're about to learn the first one.

We sat in my office one day discussing Betty's financial life. She was a successful, energetic woman with a good income who hadn't yet thought through how her money was going to work for her.

"So, Betty," I began, "I'm now going to tell you about an elegant and understated approach so you will be able to turn around your situation—to stop draining your salary and start making your money grow for you. It's one of my secret jewels."

Betty perked up, sitting straight in her chair. "But, Joan," she interjected, "I thought you said there were no 'secrets,' no 'hot tips.' You're making me nervous talking about secrets."

I laughed and touched her arm for reassurance. "Well, it's secret only because people ignore it—and it's something few people talk about. If you can manage your money so you can pay your bills each month, then you really already know the secret. Deep down, everybody knows this stuff, and yet you'll never hear about it from Wall Street."

"Okay," said Betty. "What's the great revelation?"

There are three guideposts to financial success:

1. *Spend less than you earn.*
2. *Invest the difference.*
3. *Reinvest all your returns for compounded growth until you have*

a pot of invested money that generates the income you want for life—your "trust fund."

"Here's another way to think of it, Betty. Run your life like a business so that you make a personal profit at the end of the year. Then keep socking away that profit until you have enough money to make you independent for life. That's the way to grow money, the same way any successful corporation stays in business," I said.

Betty sat in silence for a moment, considering everything I'd said. Then she glowed, a big smile dancing across her face.

"It's so simple," she said, "and it does make sense."

Yes, it *is* simple, and the specifics of investing and growing your money will be our discussion in the rest of this book.

For now, the important thing to remember is this: You can take charge of your financial life—and you can start now.

3

The White Knight Myth:
Investment Misconceptions
and Fears

The White Knight Myth
The Market Savvy Myth
The Myth of the Big Bundle
The Credit Card Myth
The Social Security/Pension Myth
The Tax Myth
The Femininity Myth

*I*n the late 1980s, I uprooted myself and moved my business from Philadelphia to California. I called upon my courage to make this change, but I did so because I thought a fuller life was possible.

The career spoke of my Wheel of Life was humming with success. My firm, Perry Investments, was widely known in "muni" bond circles, and it was one of the joys of my life. Not only was I proud that I had helped to alter the perception of what women were capable of doing in the investment industry, but I was also living a very good lifestyle. I was alone, but independent. And I was ready again to build a relationship with a man and enrich the social spoke of my Wheel. Life was indeed good, I concluded, and nothing could possibly ruin this wonderful sense of well-being I had created.

Then I fell in love.

It was like strolling through the pages of a fairy tale. He was my

Prince Charming—sexy, intelligent, romantic, amusing, generous, wealthy. And I was his princess. He surprised me with glittering gems and dazzled me with delicious dinners at four-star restaurants. We jetted on his plane to distant and exotic vacation spots. He showered me with flowers, gave me his full attention, and told me that he was truly, madly, deeply in love with me. He was magical. Surely, I assumed, he would take care of me for life. After all, he told me that he couldn't imagine life without me, and he even said he wanted to have children with me. So I eased into an illusion of security, taking for granted that he would always be there to support me.

I became financially dependent on this man, without fully realizing that I was. I used my cash to decorate my house and body, while he spent his to indulge me. And because I was so deeply into this fairy tale, I invested $30,000 in a "great" real estate venture he started. Talk about love and money being mixed up in the brain!

Being with this man was very comfortable because he paid for everything and he relieved the pressure I faced from my focus on earning money. But I didn't realize the personal cost of what I was doing, because, when he later jilted me, I was unprepared. While I was becoming intoxicated with my storybook life, he changed his mind, met someone else, and stopped dating me. After two years my Sir Lancelot mounted his steed and rode off into the sunset with his new Guinevere, and I was left flapping in the breeze!

Worse yet, I got my mother to invest in his real estate deal—another cardinal sin, because it's never a good idea to encourage family members to invest in risky projects. When the so-called love of my life went on to a new sweetheart, not only did I have the misery of getting over the relationship, but I continued to have a financial connection to him. Needless to say, the investment was also a total loss.

Anger erupted like Mount Saint Helens, and I seethed for what seemed an interminable time. For weeks I prodded myself to discover what I was so mad about. I finally understood that I was angry not so much at my ex-partner as at myself for giving up the directorship of my life. Is love about losing yourself—losing who you really are and what you stand for in life? I don't think so. Here I was, an intelligent, independent woman who had hung with the best of them on Wall Street and was now running her own business. Yet, in a blink, I'd relinquished control of my financial future by thinking my true love would be responsible for me.

I remember walking on the beach one misty day, cloaking myself in the anonymity of the fog, and thinking about how imbalanced my Wheel of Life had suddenly become. Sure, he had dumped me, but what barbed the dart even more was knowing that I had lapsed into unconsciousness and expected him to provide the security I sought in life by taking care of my long-term financial well-being. I wanted him to handle the pieces of my life that I didn't want to touch, such as taking care of my money life. And I falsely thought he could manage my financial life better than I could—that was part of what had attracted me to him in the first place. The realization struck like a thunderbolt. How could a woman as well prepared as I was still expect a man to take control of her financial future? I wondered, "Can love really be pure if it is tied up with needing financial security? What am I supposed to give him in return for financial security? And how does this relate to our souls?"

What did I think I was going to get out of that kind of relationship? What I thought I'd get was the chance to sail along without having to put any energy into some critical areas of my life; I thought I was going to get by easily. But I achieved nothing and lost a great deal. While I was busy bathing myself in fairy dust and listening to my Prince Charming croon his words of love, I missed out on nurturing my soul. I also lost some self-esteem and the opportunity to grow because I didn't accept responsibility for a major part of my life. The woman who is totally dependent on a man when it comes to money, and ignorant of her financial life, is compromising true love and paralyzing herself in the process.

THE WHITE KNIGHT MYTH

I had fallen victim to the White Knight Syndrome. And my failed love affair told me just how deeply ingrained this syndrome was. If I could hold on to this false notion for so long—the way Cinderella held claim to her glass slipper—and find it so firmly embedded in my thinking, I wondered what other women were doing. I decided right then and there that equipping myself with a plan so that I could be assured of my future well-being was essential to my ability to choose freely and negotiate my relationships throughout my life. It's vital to every woman's freedom to know her money life and to assume some control over it. Yet a 1996 Merrill Lynch study found that 42 percent of the women surveyed would rather have someone else manage their financial future than do it themselves. Only 28 percent of the men felt that way.

Do you still believe you don't have to worry about your financial life because your husband is there to take care of you? And if you're not married or partnered, do you think that someone—probably a man—will come along and handle all your money matters so that you'll never, ever have to worry? If you harbor these notions, then you're a true believer in the White Knight. He's the hero who rides up on his stalwart steed with flowing mane and sweeps the princess—you—into his arms and away to his castle, where he will see to your every need.

The White Knight Syndrome has single-handedly made a vast number of women financial cripples. It's a belief system that prevents us from moving forward and controlling our own destinies, a malaise that can rob us of our financial well-being, security, and opportunity for a quality relationship. And the White Knight takes no prisoners—the syndrome cuts across all economic, educational, age, and social lines. Beware. He comes in many guises: friend, lover, husband, partner, business associate, banker, broker, teacher, employer, father, brother, uncle, cousin, son, nephew, grandson.

The notion that women need and sometimes expect someone to take care of them isn't new. It's been documented over the decades and is deeply buried in our psyches and reinforced in our society. It's something that originates in childhood and clings to us throughout adulthood. Unfortunately, the White Knight Syndrome is a precarious cultural setup for women, one that erodes our natural growth.

Portraits of White Knight sufferers abound.

June Mendoza, the Michigan housewife I met at the Ranch, offers a vivid profile. She is someone who doesn't want to consider that women have any financial power at all. As you can see by the way she dismissed our hot-tub discussion—it was something that didn't concern her—June's mind is, for the moment at least, very closed. She is a woman who lives a life that can go on only as long as her husband's paycheck arrives on time. She basically depends on her husband—that White Knight again—to take care of her. But if he drops out of her life tomorrow—say, by a sudden death—she's going to have a problem, even with a fat insurance payoff. Statistically, women who receive life insurance proceeds go through the money in two years, and the benefits are rarely enough to care for a woman for the rest of her life.

But I do believe June showed a glimmer of curiosity back at the Ranch. She was spurred to do more with her life. Even going to the Ranch was a big step for her, because it was the first time she had ever gone on a vacation without her husband or children.

Then there's Linette Atwood, the marketing specialist from New York who is in the midst of a divorce. We became friends at the Ranch and stayed in touch after I returned to California and she to New York. I found her after she left my talk at the Ranch. I was concerned that something I'd said had resonated deeply. This was true: Talking about my divorce and my financial naïveté had cut a little too close to Linette's exposed nerve. We talked later that night. I'm going to tell you Linette's story because she is the quintessential White Knight victim. See if there's a part of you that can relate to Linette.

Linette met Marshall, her husband, after she graduated from college, and they were married a year later. Linette had grown up in a fairly traditional home: Her mother was a housewife whose interests were raising her children and working as a volunteer at a homeless shelter at their church; her father was a pharmacist who managed all the family's money matters. Linette's parents were very proud when she graduated from college, but they were more excited when she got married because, in their minds, she would now be "taken care of."

It was easy for Linette to drift into this way of thinking, and easier still to pursue her career in marketing while Marshall handled all the "dirty" work: paying the bills, picking insurance plans, doing the banking, and managing the family investments. Linette lived in a beautiful co-op on fashionable Central Park West in Manhattan, had a lovely beach house in Sag Harbor on Long Island, played tennis, traveled, dressed beautifully, and had plenty of credit cards. But she didn't know what Marshall earned or what they spent until it was too late.

"I picked up the mail before he did one day and decided to read the American Express bill because I had returned a few mail-order items and I wanted to make sure we got the credit. That's when I saw the balance. We were two payments behind and owed more than $10,000. I was shocked. I didn't know Marshall wasn't paying the bills, and I certainly didn't know how much he was spending," Linette said. "I know this sounds irresponsible or perhaps even dumb, but I never bothered to read our credit card bills before that time. I would turn over my paycheck to Marshall and let him handle it from there."

Linette was a victim of both her own stylish life and the White Knight Syndrome. The social and career spokes of her Wheel of Life were strong, but the financial and family spokes were off balance. Now Marshall is leaving her for a younger woman, a model whose face taunts Linette from the pages of many fashion magazines.

And worse, besides squandering money on expensive trinkets, Marshall made some risky real estate investments. By the time Linette filed for divorce, their net worth had declined sharply.

Linette knew she had earned a respectable amount of money during their marriage and thought she would get a sizable chunk of cash from the investments Marshall had made. Instead, there wasn't much. Besides, Marshall had kept all investments in his name only!

Linette wept the night we talked. She told me she was embarrassed, hurt, and very frightened. For years, she had lived with a false security, trusting in her White Knight to care for her future. Now she was living on a fault line, and for the moment, she had a legal thicket to hack her way through before she could even consider doing anything about her troubled finances or dream about a secure financial future.

She is accustomed to a lifestyle she has no basis for maintaining on her own. Plus she has her child to think about. She could probably work twice as hard and climb even higher up the corporate ladder. Her other option could be to perpetuate the White Knight Syndrome and marry again so someone else can take care of her. Only, this time, she will possibly have to give up love in order to reinstate what she grew up believing was security.

Linette is a graphic example of a woman whose Cinderella beliefs set her up for a major fall. Sadly, she did not understand all the real choices that money presents. Nor did she realize her full powers as a woman. What will happen to Linette? Will she be able to balance her Wheel of Life?

Maggie O'Neal, the twenty-five-year-old photographer's assistant from New Orleans, offers a variation on the White Knight theme. She may lament her credit card debt, but she nevertheless spends every dollar she earns and refuses to save because, as she's confided to close friends, she figures that, eventually, she'll marry or live with a guy, and he'll take care of her financially.

Maggie has gone through her young adulthood surfing from one relationship to another. She lived with one man for six months. He paid the rent and all the household expenses, while she shopped for herself. When the magic of new love wore off, he ended the relationship and told Maggie she was fiscally irresponsible. He was right. She is. And her parents don't help by constantly bailing her out. Interestingly, she had had no intention of attending my presentation because, she told me later, "That investment stuff is lame." But she was so intrigued by what the other women were saying in the hot tub about caring for their futures that it tweaked her curiosity.

Maggie is young and can extricate herself from the White Knight's thrall. She can begin to nurture her spirit and learn about long-term financial well-being. If she doesn't, she's in danger not only of becoming destitute when she's older, but also of trading her soul. In the process, she will have lost two spokes on her Wheel of Life: the financial and the spiritual.

Even Betty Scott, the San Francisco lawyer who comes across as fairly independent, is tainted by the White Knight. We discussed the syndrome one day and she smiled sheepishly and said, "Yep. There's a small, deeply hidden part of me that still thinks the man of my dreams will take care of me for the rest of my life so I won't have to." Fortunately, Betty has sliced through the White Knight's blue haze and made the first step toward personal financial control.

Once you untangle the White Knight myth, love and money will no longer be codependents. Whether you're single or married, working inside or outside the home, it's up to you to know about money matters and to be in charge of your finances. And with this understanding, you will easily wash that man-knight right out of your hair. But for some women, that shampoo and rinse might take a while because the White Knight is too deeply ingrained in their psyches.

I've met female clients in their forties and fifties who had not saved any money or considered their financial future because they still believed their husband, lover, employer, or even children would work out things for them in the future. And what's interesting is that many of their children really do anticipate providing for their parents. A 1996 survey by Yankelovich Partners, Phoenix, found that more than a third of the people polled who were living in households in which at least one person earned more than $40,000 a year expected to provide financial assistance to their parents.

History of the White Knight

How did the White Knight gain steam and become so powerful? From the historical roles of men and women in just about every culture in the world. For centuries, the only way a woman could gain access to real economic prosperity was through a man; thus many women depended on their beauty, prowess, and sexual attraction to achieve financial security. Women who had accumulated wealth were rich because they inherited money or married into it, not because they had earned it. This began to change over the past two decades, as women forged ahead in professions once closed to them.

The White Knight Syndrome has also been reinforced by popular culture. Women growing up in the fifties, sixties, and early seventies were surrounded by images—on television, in advertisements, and in films—that constantly told them they could sit back and allow someone else to carry the load. In *Leave It to Beaver*, who made the financial decisions in Beaver's home? Certainly not his mother, June. Who went out to work and took care of Margaret and the kids in *Father Knows Best*? The title says it all. In *All in the Family*, Edith Bunker depended totally on Archie to look after all her financial needs. And did Mrs. Brady in *The Brady Bunch* figure she'd have to do anything to ensure her financial future, other than merging her brood of three with her husband's trio of sons? Even Betty Rubble and Wilma Flintstone in *The Flintstones* were victims of the White Knight, albeit a Stone Age version. Society supported these images, which today are obsolete and cannot possibly guide a woman as she seeks financial well-being.

Meanwhile, advertising continues to target the "housewife"—the happy spender who does all the household shopping for the family and her husband. Men are perceived as the breadwinners—they come home to a clean house, clean clothes, and a nice meal, and women depend financially on these men. When you look at TV commercials, who do you find doing the laundry or plowing through supermarket aisles or packing all the neighborhood kids off with bottles of soft drinks? That's because women in our society have traditionally taken the role of buying articles that depreciate, like food and clothing, while men have been buying objects that appreciate, like stocks and collectibles.

According to Madison Avenue, the majority of women in the United States spend their time caring for a house and family and do not go outside their homes to work. That, of course, is not the case and hasn't been true for decades. In the United States, most women—60 percent, according to the U.S. Bureau of the Census—work. And when advertisers do target the professional woman, what do you see? A car advertisement telling a prospective female customer she should purchase that sparkling automobile because it's an "investment." Not! That car won't provide any income for her when she's not working, so it is in no way an investment. It's a form of transportation. Period.

Other Myths and Misconceptions

The White Knight hasn't been the only obstacle to women gaining their financial freedom. It's perhaps more pervasive because it is an emotional or psychological deterrent. But for generations a fistful of other myths and misconceptions has worked against women taking this very important next step in their liberation.

Here's a sampling of some of the most common investment falsehoods. See how many of them you've believed.

- *The Market Savvy Myth:* Smart investing requires that you become an expert in the stock market, that you follow individual companies and develop a clear sense of what and when to buy and sell.
- *The Myth of the Big Bundle:* You need a lot of money in order to invest productively.
- *The Credit Card Myth:* You need to pay off your credit cards before you can invest.
- *The Social Security/Pension Myth:* You don't have to worry about your future because Social Security, a company pension, or some other program will always be there.

- ■ *The Tax Myth:*   Your taxes will be lower when you stop working.
- ■ *The Femininity Myth:*   Competent investing isn't very feminine; it draws on qualities and skills that don't come naturally
  to women.

I frequently hear this thinking from clients and friends when
they are justifying their financial inactivity to me. But how did we
come to believe these falsehoods? Actually, it was easy, because we
haven't really stopped to consider what went into the development
of these myths.

But if you continue to wallow in the investment-myth swamp,
you're going to sink. Government statistics tell us that more than 90
percent of the women in the United States will either remain single
or be widowed or divorced at some point in their lives. Unlike our
parents or grandparents, you can no longer rely on your employer
to take care of you because fewer and fewer companies have huge
pension plans for their workers. The reality is that you're going to
have to be the caretaker of your financial future, and for the first
time in history, what you have is what you're going to have to secure
your future.

Yet with this responsibility of caring for your financial future
comes great opportunity. Never before in history have women been
able to take control of their money lives. This moment is inspira-
tional, not fearful; joyful, not filled with regrets, because it represents newfound freedom and a deepening sense of who we are. But
in order to take your place in history and to be part of a financial
revolution for women, you'll want to discard the myths that are still
in place, despite the changes that have occurred for women in our
society.

THE MARKET SAVVY MYTH

Many women have expressed feeling guilty and apologetic for not having mastered investing. I can almost rattle off the gibberish before a client does: "This is too complicated for me to understand." "I don't do numbers." "I just mastered my checkbook, and now you want me to do this?" "I majored in English and never expected to do financial stuff." "You know, I get all these millions and millions of pieces of paper from brokerage people, and I can't sort it all out. I get confused."

Face it, we aren't talking about quantum physics here, and you don't need an advanced degree in mathematics or economics in order to understand your investments. Instead, start simple. I often say, "Start with three good mutual funds and put your money in." Once you've decided on these funds, find out what you're paying for them. As time passes, compare the purchase price to their current price, and each quarter, keep track of how they've grown. And when you understand the three funds and get really good at keeping up with your investments, you might want to add some more. It's really that simple.

If you have a bunch of investments that are all over the map, pare them down to four or six—a small number you can handle and easily track. I'll be discussing the mechanics of mutual fund investing in Chapter 7. Right now, the basic lesson is straightforward: Investing doesn't have to be complicated.

Certainly, knowledge and a little study can't hurt and could prove to be very helpful. It's always good to inform yourself before taking on any situation, whether it's a trip to the doctor, a job interview, or an appearance in traffic court. But it isn't necessary to go back to school to learn how to invest. I partner with my clients, working out with them a personal investment strategy based on their needs and financial picture. I then encourage them to make their own choices, be guided by their own knowledge, and trust in themselves. That way, they can ride out the market dips and have long-term conviction as they surf their investment waves into the future.

THE MYTH OF THE BIG BUNDLE

I can't begin to tell you how many people ask me, "Do you require people to invest a minimum amount of money before you will work with them?" I tell them no, and I emphasize also that it doesn't matter how rich they are or even how old. The point is to develop momentum from wherever you are. It's better to start young, but having some money when you're older is better than having none at all.

How young is young? Let me tell you about my stepson, Sean. When he was eleven years old, he set up a lemonade stand in our driveway during our town's annual summer arts fairs, which take place on our street in the downtown area—called Old Town—of Los Gatos. Easily more than a thousand people attend, and many found their way to Sean's stand. Sean used his own money to purchase cases of lemons—at wholesale prices—at the farmer's market, and my husband took Sean to Price Club to buy paper cups and sugar. And because the arts fairs are hot, thirsty events, Sean could charge $1.50 a glass for the cold drinks.

Sean found that he could earn nearly $500 for each of the three weekends he was in business during four summers of street festivals. We have a family agreement that 50 percent of Sean's earnings will go to a mutual fund he selected; he can spend the other 50 percent. His mutual fund has flourished to about $3,500 from his investment and its growth. Two years from now, when Sean turns sixteen, he'll have enough in his mutual fund to buy a used car. He's learning the investing steps and will surely take good care of a car he has purchased with his own money.

Sean is so proud of his investments that he spread the gospel to my two little nieces, aged nine and eleven. The girls visited me not so long ago, and I took them shopping at F.A.O. Schwarz in San Francisco. I gave them each $100 to spend. Well, the older one, Katie, announced in the toy store that she was going to spend only half of her money and that she didn't want to go a penny over because she wanted me to take the other half and start a mutual fund just like Sean's. My other niece, Molly, quickly piped up and said, "Me, too."

Last summer, two little girls down the street started their own weekend lemonade stand during the neighborhood festival. They, too, charged $1.50 a glass. A few days later, I ran into the girls on the street, and I paused to ask the older of the two, who looked to be about nine years old, whether they had had fun selling lemonade. She said they did. I asked if they'd made money, and she told me that she and her cousin had earned $200 for the weekend.

I said, "That's great. That's a lot of money. Did you save some of it?"

"Oh, no. We wouldn't know how to do that. We don't do that in my family," she responded candidly with big, blue, wide eyes. "We just put the money in our pockets and buy whatever we want."

"Well, maybe you could try saving some and maybe turn that into a lot more," I said, trying to encourage a little financial education in the young.

Once again she replied, "We just don't do that in our family, and besides, my cousin's already spent her $100. I have mine in my pocket to buy whatever I want."

Unfortunately, here's a girl whose family remains mired in old beliefs, and she's unlikely to begin saving and investing at a really young age, as Sean and my nieces did. But she has years yet before her investing time becomes critical. Let's hope she'll one day tuck at least half of that hundred bucks into a mutual fund instead of her pocket.

Wall Street put out the myth that you need thousands of dollars in order to dabble with investments. It's in its own interest, because large investments generate large commissions. But as you can see from Sean and my nieces, anyone can get in the game—and with any amount of money. The same principles apply whether you have a big bundle or a small stash.

Lisa, Maggie O'Neal's twenty-four-year-old roommate, was also adrift in the credit card bog, literally living from paycheck to paycheck. She had been working for about two years for a software company since graduating from college and knew her money was slipping away. Maggie told her about my talk after she returned from the Ranch, and Lisa called me.

As we spoke, she felt she could hold on to $100 from her paycheck. A hundred dollars, though, wasn't even enough to get a piggy bank excited, she thought. But it is. With that money, she can open a brokerage account and put it into a money market fund. With a little patience, she can watch her fund grow until she has enough money to move into other investments. Or, I suggested to her, she can join an investment club, an increasingly popular option for women who want to get started in investing. Many such clubs have monthly dues of just $50. With the support of other women in the club, she could learn more about investing, and they can help her make decisions about money matters.

Lisa decided to do both. She started a money market account and found an investment club to join. Now Lisa is on her way to sound investment strategies, and perhaps she will be a solid influence on Maggie.

THE CREDIT CARD MYTH

Credit cards, the Draculas of the financial world, drain assets out of our lives at an alarming rate. Put another way, a credit card is like a cheeseburger: It's full of fat (interest), clogs your arteries (debt), and makes you feel sluggish, and it adds nothing to your general health.

And like fast-food burgers, credit cards are slickly marketed. As soon as women entered the workforce in large numbers, banks launched massive campaigns to target these wonderful new consumers and offered credit cards—sometimes free of charge. With plastic in hand, women took shopping to new and glorious heights. Credit card companies taught us lessons about spending, such as the notion that "if something isn't new, it isn't good." Do you want to know just how much we've been spending with our credit cards?

According to the Consumer Federation of America, we charged more than $1 trillion in 1996 alone, and credit card debt—including interest—exceeded $400 billion. Some people have more racked up on their credit card balances than they earn in a year or even two years, and credit cards have been a primary factor in the alarming increase of personal bankruptcies.

It's time to rethink our spending habits and begin to evaluate what we buy and what we choose to do in life based on lasting values—the joy or peace we derive from a possession or an activity—and not just on the momentary thrill of spending. For example, instead of spending a lot of money to go skiing, why not take out your bike and go for a long ride with a friend, your husband, or your family? Think of the stress you'll avoid: You won't have to worry about packing and rushing to an airport or driving long hours to the nearest slope.

Similarly, maybe you'd choose not to go to a stadium to watch a football game and have to deal with traffic, crowds, and possibly bad weather—to say nothing of exorbitant prices for tickets, food, drinks, parking, and souvenirs—when you can watch the same game in the comfort of your home with a bunch of friends.

In short, forget what credit card companies—and a million consumer-oriented television commercials—have taught you. Vote to simplify your life and make "fun" and "inexpensive" virtues, and avoid "costly" and "stressful."

And consider this: While credit card companies were encouraging us to spend, how many women were saving or investing? Not too many. Women today are earning more than they've ever earned, and some are catching up with men. But women buy more than men and save half as much. When they do save, it's usually for major purchases: a vacation, a home-remodeling job, jewelry, or a child's education. In the meantime, they take the plastic and slide into debt.

The worst credit cards are the high-interest bankcards, such as MasterCard and Visa. Unless you pay off the balance each month, you're stuck with excessive interest as well as the principal from your charges. And now some credit cards are proposing to charge you a fee if you pay off your balance each month!

Many banks are now offering lower interest rates for their MasterCards and Visas and are encouraging cardholders to consolidate charges from old cards onto a new one. This can help as long as you take two crucial steps: (1) Never again use the higher-rate card, and (2) make a commitment not to run up a large balance on the lower-rate card.

But that seldom works for credit card junkies. Here's what happens: You leave home with a virgin card—no charges. You feel invincible, full of power. With card in hand, you can go anywhere in the world and buy anything you want (within your limit if you have one). After all, that's what all the glamour ads on television tell you.

The only problem is, you start to lose track of what you've been racking up because a credit card is like play money. All of a sudden, you're in debt and all your other financial responsibilities take a tumble as well as you try to deflate the credit card balloon.

Soon you think it's hopeless, that you'll never emerge from credit card hell, and investing is the last thing on your mind. That's how Maggie feels.

I suggest not using bankcards *unless you pay in full each month.* Instead, use American Express or Diners Club—a card whose balance you must pay in full with each statement—and pay with cash as much as possible. It is a myth that you need a credit card. When yours is full, you can go for months without using one, and by paying cash, you can more easily keep track of your spending. And, yes, it's possible to avoid credit cards altogether. You can rent a car and stay in the best hotels by paying cash—you'll just be required to put down a hefty deposit, which will be returned to you when you pay your bill.

The twenty-first-century thing to do, though, is to use a debit card. A debit card looks and feels like a credit card, and companies like Citibank and your local bank are issuing them. You can rent a car, stay in a hotel, eat in your favorite restaurant, buy airline tickets, shop in any store. But with the debit card, you can spend only as much money as you have in the bank because the cost of your purchase is immediately deducted from your checking account.

With a debit card, you won't be paying off credit card bills—you'll be spending your own money. You'll also have a better sense of reality about your financial life because what you spend is *yours* and not plastic "play money." Just remember, though, that while you're out shopping, the money you're spending from your account also has to be used to meet other obligations, such as rent or mortgage, transportation, utilities, and whatnot. You can't falsely assume you have a credit line, because you don't. What you have is a checking balance. Use your debit card to spend within, not beyond, your means, as so many people fail to do with credit cards.

Used the right way, a debit card can lead you down the path of "spend less than you earn and invest the difference"—the first of our financial jewels. Plus, you may also find extra cash in your pocket because you won't be paying those exorbitant interest charges of 20 percent plus that come with credit cards. If you don't like to carry around large sums of cash, and if you don't have a debit card, sign up for one.

But if you stick with credit cards, I suggest that you *not* wait until you've paid off your card debts before you begin investing. Why? Because it's easy to stay stuck in the cycle of never being able to pay off your credit cards, and so you put off investing forever. Besides, for many women, it doesn't "feel good" to pay off credit cards—it's an obligation, not a joy. But it does feel good to invest, because you know you're building your future, and that's sweet. My wish is for you to have the psychic reward of seeing your savings and brokerage account balances grow each month as soon as possible. I think that once you've experienced this, you'll be hooked for life.

THE SOCIAL SECURITY/PENSION MYTH

In my parents' generation, when people retired, most employers provided them with some lifetime income. My father is an example.

He worked as a hospital administrator. He had a pension plan plus substantial savings from the income he earned during his career. So he knew that he and my mother would be able to live comfortably once he retired. Similarly, my father-in-law worked for Sears, Roebuck, and his company assisted employees with financial planning and pension plans. Today he enjoys a comfortable retirement.

Unfortunately, this practice has gone the way of vinyl records and black-and-white TV sets. Just look at Silicon Valley, the mammoth computer and electronics industrial center. It is one of the hottest areas of economic growth in America. Yet only a few companies in Silicon Valley have traditional pension plans. The others are more likely to offer 401(k) plans, in which employees actively participate in making investments and managing their invested dollars, and they have no guarantee of future income.

Other workplace trends are diminishing our financial security, too. In 1974, I worked for the state treasurer's office in Nashville, Tennessee. One employee came to work each day, sat at his empty desk, and read *The Wall Street Journal.* He had been appointed to his position by a political friend. He had absolutely no job responsibilities and could not be fired. And I've heard similar stories from people in private business—tales of "Old Bill," who never did any work but coasted toward retirement thanks to a lenient or friendly boss. Back then, even less-than-hardworking employees could usually expect their employers to be there for them.

Well, kiss those sweet days good-bye. Today, there is no place in the United States where you can go sit and have long-term job security; foreign competition and the heightened scramble for profits in every industry have made sure of that.

Furthermore, even for those who have steady jobs, corporations are no longer in the business of guaranteeing your job and long-term financial security. There are several reasons for this. To begin with, the federal government has made pension and qualified plan rules so complicated and the administration of these plans so costly that many employers no longer want to offer them. To make matters worse, some firms have badly mismanaged pension funds and have been hit with lawsuits from angry employees who lost their pensions. In one such instance, an executive used the company's pension funds, purchased numerous paintings by LeRoy Neiman, and hung them in his house. So cash was not available in the plan as employees needed it.

As of 1995, the Department of Labor was investigating more than three hundred companies accused of looting their employees' savings. The 401(k) plans are particularly vulnerable to all sorts of fraud, and not much can be done once the funds are gone because these plans are not federally insured.

Just as employer pension plans have slowly evaporated, Social Security has become beleaguered. Initiated as a ray of hope for Americans who would otherwise starve in their old age, Social Security has mutated into an almost unmanageable monolith that in 1994 paid out almost $25.3 billion to about seven million people. But with the first crop of baby boomers—the largest aging population in the history of this country—heading for retirement in thirteen years, it is greatly feared that the Social Security trust fund will be empty. All the money you contributed during your working years— easily more than $50,000 for the average person—is cash you might never see. Many baby boomers realize that they won't be able to depend on Social Security to survive and that they will need to continue working well into their seventies and even eighties in order to maintain their current lifestyles and financially support themselves.

When you combine pension woes with the fact that few people actually save money, the enormity of the problem is evident.

The United States has the lowest savings rate of all the industrialized nations; only half of those who work actually save, according to a study by Merrill Lynch. Women are especially lax in this area. The Merrill Lynch study showed that only 26 percent of the women questioned were saving for their future, while 29 percent were saving for their children's education, 27 percent were buying cars or making home improvements, and 9 percent were saving for a vacation.

When those wage earners grow older, their lack of savings, coupled with less job security and a lost income, will push some into poverty. Eighty percent of the population retires below the poverty level, and 70 percent of the elderly poor in America are women. Sadly, many of these women were once part of the middle class and led affluent or comfortable lives.

Our parents worked hard, saved, and built as good a life as they could for their children, and if they were fortunate and planned carefully, they left work on good pensions, Social Security benefits, and whatever investments they had made along the way. Many baby boomers have yet to think about their nonworking years, and because we live longer than men, women in particular are at a critical juncture in addressing their financial concerns. And with so many women today deferring childbearing or not having children at all, the issue of who will care for us if we can't care for ourselves is a real concern.

This all means that we're going to have to be solely responsible for our financial futures. The state of your financial health is up to you.

And you know what? That's a wonderful prospect, because it means that women finally have claimed their seat in economic America! Let me repeat, women are *finally* staking their own claim in their own future.

THE TAX MYTH

Many retirement plans are based on the assumption that your financial needs will drastically diminish when you ease out of working. One of the major reasons for this assumption is the belief that income tax becomes negligible when your working days are over.

If you believe that when you stop working, you won't have to pay taxes because you won't be earning a salary, don't count on it. If you've managed to accumulate, say, $100,000 in an IRA over the years, you'll be paying ordinary taxes on that cash when you withdraw it. Depending on where you live, you'll probably end up with only about half of your $100,000 once you factor in state and federal taxes. This is true whether you have an IRA, a Keogh, or a 401(k) plan. I'll show you exactly how these qualified plans work in Chapter 6. Social Security benefits are also taxed, and the rate and level of these taxes will likely increase over the next decade as lawmakers scramble to find ways to protect the solvency of the U.S. Treasury against the unprecedented demands of baby boomers and federally mandated programs.

Therefore, if you want to keep the same lifestyle that you now have, and if you don't want to cut back on any of the things that give you joy or simply make life a little easier, you'll need to receive the same income that you now have—and then some. Thus, you'll be in the same tax bracket that you are in now—or perhaps you'll be in an even higher one if taxes go up in the future.

THE FEMININITY MYTH

Some women—and some men, too, of course—believe that investing is a man's game; they believe it is not very "feminine." Of course, the way we are brought up is a major reason for such myths. As we've already seen, most girls aren't taught much about money by their parents. And what they do learn at home is often oriented more toward spending than toward saving and investing. Although men's financial education is far from ideal, it tends to be far better than women's.

If a woman received any sound financial advice at all when she was young, it probably was to start a savings account when she began working and to add a little to it from each paycheck. Nothing wrong there. Except today, with interest rates so low, a savings account is not a good way to grow cash. A simple alternative might be a money market fund. But that sounds too complicated to some women, and so they stay with the lower-interest-bearing savings account. I mean, how many people actually go out and say, "I'm going to open a brokerage account with a money market fund and start doing some serious saving here"? Very few. Unless you know how to open a brokerage account—an investment account that is similar to a checking account—it's easier to blow it off.

Other stereotypes feed the problem. For example, schools tend to shortchange girls, especially when it comes to math. Gender bias in schools has been well documented by both educational and governmental agencies and widely reported over the years in the media. In a hundred subtle and not-so-subtle ways, most schools discourage girls from pursuing high achievement in mathematics or economics. Counselors steer girls to "easier" subjects, like English literature or home economics (translation: cooking tuna casserole), and teachers often fail to call on girls for answers or encourage girls to participate actively in math classes. Math scores for the Scholastic Achievement Test (SAT) mirror the imbalance. In 1995, boys averaged 503, while girls averaged 463. Even Mattel, the toy company, unthinkingly reinforced the problem by recently creating a talking Barbie doll programmed to complain, "Math class is hard!" (Fortunately, protests by women scientists and mathematicians forced Mattel to alter Barbie's message.)

Why does all this matter? Let's face it—investing is, in part, a numbers game. You don't need trigonometry or calculus to manage your personal finances, but if you become anxious at the very sight of a column of figures, you're likely to transfer some of that anxiety to investing. So when a young woman who has been discouraged from learning math grows up, she sometimes grouses about balancing her checkbook and often turns to her father, husband, or companion for help with her financial decisions. This is even borne out by statistics. A 1996 survey by OppenheimerFunds found that 66 percent of the women questioned said that investing was "too complicated."

Of course, the stereotypical belief that investing isn't feminine is completely false—a relic of the tainted old days. It's like saying that a woman who plays sports is not feminine, or that a female who practices law or flies in a space shuttle is less of a woman. As role models like Jackie Joyner-Kersee, Sandra Day O'Connor, and Sally

Ride have shown us, just the opposite is true. Each is more of a woman because she's expressing herself more fully.

I found myself attending a seminar in Michigan a few months after my trip to the Ranch. There was a cocktail party for the participants, and June Mendoza, who had shown little interest in financial matters when we met at the Ranch, was there with her husband, Steve. We were happy to see one another and began chatting.

I could sense that June was a little on edge. I thought perhaps her daughter Ellie, who had been battling an eating disorder, was in trouble again. But this was not the case. It seemed that our encounter at the Ranch had had a greater influence on June's thinking than I'd imagined. She was percolating with change—or at least the *idea* of change—but was frustrated because part of herself remained trapped in old thinking. June steered me away from the group we were in; we huddled close to a wall so we could talk more privately.

"Look," she began somewhat tentatively, "I don't know if I should be talking to you about our family business. Deep down, I guess it isn't something a woman needs to be involved in."

My eyebrows rose. "Why is that, June?"

"Well, you know," she said, peeking over her shoulder to make sure no one was listening. "It's so . . . so . . . well, I just think investing is something I shouldn't have to do."

I knew it would take time to convince June otherwise, so I invited her to lunch the next day so that we could speak at length. But she declined.

"What are you so concerned about?" I asked gently.

After a long silence, June replied, "Frankly, I'm not so sure I like the way my husband is handling our money. I've thought maybe I could do it, but then I'd have to do all these things by myself. I don't know."

"Why do you think this is something you can't handle? It isn't brain surgery, you know." I laughed a little to lighten things up, but June remained solemn.

"It just *is*," she said, shaking her head. "Stocks—mutual funds—interest rates—dividends—it's too complicated. I can't do it."

"No," I replied, "what I hear you saying is that you *don't want* to do it."

Oh, poor June! It was easy to see how torn she was. She wanted it all to work out but without taking the initiative to make it happen. She wanted the bread to get baked, but she didn't want to put her hands in the dough.

But at least June was beginning to ask questions and to entertain the idea that she had other choices. I invited her to call me if she wanted to talk further.

There are many more Junes in the world—women who have lived most of their lives strongly believing that a brush with that old male bastion of finance might diminish their femininity. The wiser approach is for women to stop thinking of investing as task oriented, focused on "getting things done" and "making final decisions"—and they'd better be the *right* decisions! Instead, create a more fluid vision of investing as a potentially pleasurable process, an act of love. After all, if you think about it, looking after your financial health is a way to express your self-love, your belief that you are special and worthy of a rewarding and comfortable future.

In reality, investing is one of the most feminine things you can do. Smart investing draws on the skills and strengths considered to be classically "womanly." It requires a combination of insight and intuition, observation and feeling, concern and conviction. Some in the financial community would have us believe that investing is just too complex and mysterious for a woman to handle. Baloney! If you can run a household, organize a closet, run a Parent-Teacher Association meeting, or shop shrewdly, you can be a successful investor. If you can tough out the bad times in a relationship and have the wisdom, patience, and understanding to make a love affair or a marriage work, then you've got what it takes to generate cash for life.

Beyond the Myths

So much for these myths.

In the end, you and you alone are responsible for your financial security. You and you alone have the power to decide how to govern your money matters. Yes, there is a tremendous amount of hope for your future, but it's in your hands—it won't be realized by waiting for the White Knight to arrive or wishing that he will magically appear.

You're well on the path to learning more about managing your financial future. Having altered your thinking about the myths and misconceptions of investing, you're now more open to choosing a strategy and getting really excited about nurturing yourself with your money. No matter your circumstances, you're in a position to fix whatever hasn't been working and improve whatever has. Financial security is within your reach.

The real joy comes from knowing that you've taken charge of your destiny and that you've begun to understand the power of money and your power as a woman in these times. Everything else is a bonus.

4

The Road to Financial Fulfillment: Making Your Money Grow

The Game of Golf
Your Financial Picture
Creative Income
Planning Ahead
The "Rule of 72"

THE GAME OF GOLF

*L*et's play a game of golf.

It's a magnificent day. The sky is spectacularly blue, clear, and sunny. The air is crisp. And best of all, we have the entire course to ourselves. To make things interesting, why don't we put a wager on our game. How about $10,000 for eighteen holes?

Oh, you don't want to do that. Too steep, huh? Well, let's make it fun, then. How about 10 cents a hole? Ah, you like that. Okay. Now let's make it even more entertaining. Suppose we double the dime at each hole?

You'll go for that, too? Well, guess what? That dime, doubled eighteen times as we play our round of golf, *grows into a whopping $13,107.20*! Here's how it works:

For the first few holes, not much seems to be happening. At

the first hole, our bet is 10 cents. At the second hole, it's 20 cents. At the third hole, it's 40 cents, and at the fourth hole, it's 80 cents.

The action gets a little hotter as we move into the middle of our round of golf. At the fifth hole, our bet is $1.60. At the sixth hole, it's $3.20. At the seventh hole, it's $6.40. At the eighth hole, it's $12.80, and at the ninth hole, it's $25.60. Now we're talking about money that you'd notice if you were to lose—or win—it. But watch what happens on the back nine.

At the tenth hole, the wager is worth $51.20. At the eleventh hole, it's $102.40. At the twelfth hole, it's $204.80. At the thirteenth hole, it's $409.60, and at the fourteenth hole, it's $819.20.

What's become of the meek little dime we started with? Suddenly, you feel like a women's golf pro, competing for some serious bucks. But let's complete the course.

At the fifteenth hole, the bet is $1,638.40. At the sixteenth hole, it's $3,276.80. At the seventeenth hole, it's $6,553.60. And at the eighteenth and final hole, our bet has grown from a measly 10 cents to $13,107.20.

Suppose you were winning the bet but had to skip the last five holes because of a sudden thundershower. Your results would be very different, wouldn't they?

Our fantasy game of golf offers a good example of how quickly money can multiply when it grows at a steady rate without being disturbed. Our illustration was a wager. But imagine what a good investment could do. For example, let's say your grandparents had given you $1,000 when you were born, and your parents put it in a stock market investment that earned 12 percent per year. (That's not an unusual rate of growth for a well-managed stock portfolio, by the way.) If today were your fortieth birthday, your stock would be worth $93,051.

And if your investment earned 20 percent interest—a fine performance, but not unheard of—you'd be a forty-year-old millionaire! Invested money grows naturally over time.

So, you see, it's easy to cultivate money. And all of us have the power to plant the money seed, water it, nurture it, sit back, and watch it take root and flourish. Just picture harvest time!

But to reap that harvest, you have to take action to let your money work for you. If your money isn't working, then you're throwing it away. And if you have no control over your investments, then you are powerless to enjoy their full potential.

That was the case with Betty Scott, the San Francisco lawyer. As far as her business goes, Betty is sitting pretty. Her firm has tripled its profits over the last three years. She is secure in her job and is highly respected. She loves her work, so she is not going to quit anytime soon. And it's unlikely she will be fired. She described all these positives to me with well-deserved pride as we sat in my office and continued discussing her financial picture.

"All of that is wonderful, Betty," I said. "But there's another side to the story. The fact is, you're losing money right now, every day. By failing to set up a way for your money to work for you, you're losing the money your investments could be generating for your future. They can work even when you're not working. How are your skills with money? Have you managed to keep any in the bank as a safety net for the time when you'll stop working?"

Betty shook her head and sighed. "I don't know what it is," she said quietly. "I make a very good salary, more than I expected to be making at this point. And I keep thinking I should have been able to save a lot more money by now—I mean, I've been working at the same place for almost ten years. And believe me, I put in long, hard hours, and I don't have much of a life outside of work. But finding the time to invest is just so hard. It seems easier to keep going month by month, and to let the future take care of itself."

Betty sighed again, and so did I. It's a familiar story. Betty wasn't very different from many other women. She was using her money one month at a time to meet her obligations when, with a slight shift in perspective and spending, she would have the opportunity—as does everyone who earns a steady income—to create an investment vision that will keep her safe and solvent when she's no longer earning cash. She also had within her reach the tools to carve out a more fulfilling life for herself. Betty was young, attractive, witty, vibrant, loyal, caring, bright, and ambitious. But she was also lonely.

The dent in the financial spoke of her Wheel of Life was throwing her whole life out of balance. She was spiritually poor and fearful of relationships because she spent all her energy working or worrying about paying her bills. The men she dated tended to be less ambitious than she, and Betty wondered whether they were attracted to her or to her ability to care for them financially.

We talked about what was preventing Betty from leading a more balanced life. She agreed that the same misconceptions, fears, and myths—including the White Knight Syndrome—that hold back most women were part of her challenge. But luckily for Betty, she has awakened from her financial slumber and is beginning to give her future some serious thought. She hasn't hatched her strategy yet, but she's well on her way to making one. And, more important, Betty is overcoming a central fear she's harbored much of her life— that she'll be short of money and will not be able to take adequate care of herself. That particular fear—one shared by many women— underlies her driving work ethic. However, it had rooted her in place so that she couldn't move forward in her financial life and now *is* the time to get rid of it.

YOUR FINANCIAL PICTURE

You, too, are ready to actively plan for your future. First, though, you'll want to do some thinking about your current lifestyle and the role money plays in it. Think about what truly has value in your life—the things and people who give you joy, peace, and happiness—and what doesn't. Especially take note of what is valuable in the long run.

Let's begin by taking an inventory of your financial life. We'll use the Lifestyle Expenses worksheet provided on the next page. Grab a pencil, turn to that page, and fill in the blanks.

First: What does it currently cost you to live? In other words, how much do you need each month or each week times four to support the lifestyle you've chosen or grown accustomed to? If you're like many people, the answer to that question will be easy: your entire paycheck! Those like Maggie O'Neal need not only their entire paycheck but whatever else they can pick up from parents or friends or from a dwindling savings account.

On the other hand, you might have income beyond what you require for basic expenses, and some of that money can clearly become part of a regular wealth-building plan. In any case, take some time to think about all of the ways you currently spend money. Then list them. Be honest and as realistic as possible. To get control of your finances, you need to know where your money has been going each month so you can see what you're doing.

LIFESTYLE EXPENSES

Monthly Costs for	*Amount You're Spending* *
Food	$_____
Housing	$_____
Telephone	$_____
Utilities	$_____
Transportation	$_____
Insurance	$_____
Clothes	$_____
Entertainment	$_____
Education	$_____
Child care	$_____
Personal care, beauty	$_____
Sundries	$_____
Medical	$_____
Taxes	$_____
Total lifestyle expenses	$_____

* Ballpark the numbers. A rough but realistic total will suffice.

Second: Which, if any, of your assets create money for you? This includes anything that generates profits, interest, or income, like certificates of deposits (CDs), an interest-bearing bank account, stocks, bonds, mutual funds, a qualified retirement plan, or rental property. Fill in the numbers on the Income-Producing Assets worksheet on the next page.

Don't count as an asset anything you own that does not have the potential to produce income. Your car, for example, is not included here; neither is your house. These two items are not going to produce any income for you. That's why I call money spent for your house and your car "money in jail." The wealth they represent is stuck there; it won't provide you with cash to support you later in life.

Of course, owning a house and a car is worthwhile, even necessary, for many people. They allow you to live comfortably by providing shelter and transportation. I call them "tickets to life." Others, perhaps your children, grandchildren, and heirs, may realize cash by selling them. But as far as you're concerned, their value is locked in. The goal of owning a house and a car is to have them fully paid for by the time you're no longer working. That's a wealth-building strategy.

How about that eighteen-foot skiff you own for tooling about the bay on Sunday afternoons? When you bought it, the salesman called it "a great investment." Is the boat an income-producing asset? Nope. But if you charter it out for fishing trips or waterskiing sessions and thereby earn some income from it, it becomes so.

As for that little mountain, beachfront, or lakefront cottage you just bought, put some rent-paying tenants into it, and you'll have an asset that works for you. Otherwise it doesn't.

So, at this moment, which of your assets produce cash for you? Assuming that you envision not working someday, your objective must be to replace your salary with cash flow from income-producing assets in order to continue your current lifestyle. If you don't have any investments to begin this process, you're in trouble. If you do, you're in motion.

INCOME-PRODUCING ASSETS

Assets	Amount Invested*
Savings account	$_____
Stocks	$_____
Bonds	$_____
Income-producing real estate	$_____
IRA	$_____
401(k)	$_____
Pension plan	$_____
Keogh	$_____
Cash value in annuity	$_____
Cash value in life insurance	$_____
Other	$_____
Total Income-Producing Assets	$_____

* Ballpark the numbers. A rough but realistic total will suffice.

Freeing Yourself from Consumer Hype

Unfortunately, many people have few items on their list of income-producing assets because they fail to value long-term goals over short-term desires. They get seduced by the moment and the quick-fix feeling that a new purchase can inspire. Have you noticed that shopping can change your mood just as eating sometimes does? And advertisers and retailers certainly do their best to intensify and multiply our short-term whims.

Overconsuming may mean buying too many things. It can also mean insisting on "only the best" when buying clothes or other products. Too often, a well-intentioned quest for quality degenerates into a wasteful pursuit of prestige. A great deal of the money people used to save for their futures has gone to "labels and logos." We have been lured into thinking that we will somehow feel better about ourselves if we wear a T-shirt by Nike or a suit by Armani, if we carry a purse by Fendi, or if we drive that mean machine with an Italian name. What people might have saved in the past, they now spend to be "designered."

That was part of Betty's challenge. She had bartered her soul for labels and logos to such an extent that needless spending threatened her long-term financial security. Her credo was "If it costs a lot, it's good." She was a woman who would rather pay $200 for a small Prada knapsack than $35 for a larger no-name brand that would wear just as well. She poured out cash for the label du jour without blinking or thinking.

We've all met plenty of people with Betty's point of view. I know one woman who spent $7,500 for a wedding dress, which she wore one time and then folded away in mothballs for all eternity. Her maid of honor told her, "I'd rather spend $500 on a nice dress and invest the other $7,000 in a good mutual fund." But the woman didn't understand her friend's reasoning. Unfortunately, her attitude toward spending borders on the pathological: To cover her spending tracks, she destroys all bank statements and credit card bills so that her husband won't know how much damage she's done. This individual needs not only rewiring as far as financial planning and investing for the future are concerned, but serious counseling, because she has a labels-and-logos addiction and a profoundly serious case of irresponsibility. Maybe someday we'll have an L.L.A.—Labels and Logos Anonymous.

Sadly, our society's obsession with labels and logos doesn't stop with adults. Kids, too, are willing victims. When you agree to drop $140 on those Air Jordan sneakers your ten-year-old just "has to have," what are you teaching that child about satisfying her or his own needs? Advertising gets all of us to buy by promising to change the way we feel for the moment, and then, a second later, it encourages us to do it all over again. The emotional buying cycle induced by advertising—"Buy/Feel Good/Want/Buy Again"—is not a long-term fix for security and happiness. Take it from me, though—money working for you is.

Look closely at your spending patterns and consider how much you could save by not being seduced by a designer name or the hot item of the day. Instead of paying $75 for a sweatshirt with a trendy logo, you can buy an equally good one for $30. Rather than get soaked for $20 for a bottle of shampoo at a popular hair salon, you can pick up something just as good at your local drugstore for $2. Already, you have $63 set aside to invest. Do the same with pricier goods, like suits, dresses, shoes, sports equipment, furniture, stereo equipment, cars, and computers, and you'll see just how much you can accumulate for your own wealth building.

One more example: Why should you pay $2,000 or more a year for membership in the most popular health club in town, when you can work out on the same equipment for a few bucks at your local Y or a modest gym? If you're really serious about being in good physical shape, then it doesn't matter where you work out. Are glitz, glitter, and glamour more important than your financial future? Imagine what you can save for yourself if you cut out one or two extras.

Here's what *Fortune* magazine found: If a married couple, both forty, went to a restaurant and a movie two times a month instead of four and invested the difference, they would net more than $150,000 by age sixty-five.

As you examine your spending habits, the operative wealth-building question is: "What's really going to add joy, peace, and tranquility to my life, not just at the moment but down the road?" The trick is to keep what gives you true pleasure and enhances your being, but pare back what gives you only a false sense of status. And learn to enjoy the possessions and activities that add a little spring to your stride for what they are and not for any prestige that may be attached to them. With this positive approach, you'll free yourself from the grip of consumerism and take charge of your financial life. The more strongly we value ourselves and not an image based on someone else's standards, the better we'll be able to temper the incessant hammering of merchandising.

You have the power, then, to make some radical but necessary changes. You already have the first tool to make it happen: the first financial jewel—*"Spend less than you earn and invest the difference."* Most people ignore it. According to statistics gathered by the Federal Reserve Board in 1993, 43 percent of all American families spend more than they earn. If these statistics apply to you, plan to make a change—and do it now.

CREATIVE INCOME

If your spending plan is in place and you're still short of cash to invest, try this approach: Think about how you can generate more money through "creative" sources. How can you add more value where you work so that people will want to pay you more? What skills, talents, and resources do you have to supplement what you're already doing to increase your income? How can you think creatively about your situation so both you and others will benefit from your energy? Maybe it's simply a matter of taking a good, hard look at your work environment, finding something that could be done better, and volunteering to handle it. Then, once you've demonstrated your added value, ask to be remunerated for it. Or you might consider starting a home business or expanding the services that your business offers. If you "noodle" this—let it roll around in your mind for a while—you'll come up with something.

A woman named Jane, for example, came to see me one day. We talked at length about her lifestyle and where her money was going. Jane works for a software company and decided she could easily start a newsletter that would educate and help people using her company's software; she would provide a real benefit for which she could be paid.

Then there's Lori, who found that by simply taking long walks along the beach during low tide, she could collect sea glass—broken bits of glass from bottles, glasses, and other objects that have been transformed by the sea and sand into smooth, translucent, frosty, colored "gems"—and recycle it into beautiful jewelry. With a small investment for silver wire, she's fashioned one-of-a-kind earrings, pendants, bracelets, and brooches that fetch from $10 to $150. She's attracted a group of steady customers who look forward to buying her crafts at Christmastime to give as gifts. The money Lori makes from her jewelry designs is earmarked for her wealth-building plans and goes directly for her financial future.

And my dear friend Linda, who owns a cooking school, decided she could increase her income by selling spices, bowls, platters, pots, pans, place mats, and napkins at her school. Linda's students now happily buy flavored olive oils, herbes de Provence, and garlic presses from her so that they can create the delicious dishes she teaches them to cook.

What can you do to spice up your life for yourself and others?

I had the opportunity to apply that philosophy when Maggie made a surprise call to my office. I say "surprise" because of all the women I met at the Ranch, I never expected to hear from the irresponsible Maggie. But she had had an epiphany of sorts.

For about seven or eight months, Maggie had gone to her employer and borrowed against her next paycheck so that she could cover existing bills. Her boss handed out the cash and suffered the bookkeeping complications to oblige Maggie, whose work she valued. But the last time Maggie made the request, she had a harsh awakening.

"She said no. I couldn't believe it!" Maggie said. "She told me, 'If you ever expect to get yourself out of your money problems, you're going to have to learn how to manage your money. Stop buying junk and start saving. And stop drawing from your future paychecks.' At first, I was mad as I could be, and I stormed out of her office and ran to the phone to call my mother. I knew *she* would give me money. But something stopped me from dialing. I'm not really sure what it was, but I think my boss's rebuff was the first time anyone had ever said no to me. It was like a good, swift kick in the butt, and maybe that's just what I needed!"

So now Maggie seriously considered what she was doing and began to view it as a challenge and to think about changing it.

"Joan, I'm so frightened and confused. I don't know how to start getting myself straight," she said.

"Confusion is good," I told Maggie. "It means that your brain is considering something new and it's not yet fully integrated into your thinking. So let's work on that."

We did a quick financial inventory. I learned that Maggie had $6,500 in credit card debts; three cards had been canceled, and she was a month behind on her share of the rent and two months behind on her utilities. Any day now, she would lose her telephone service and electricity. Some immediate steps had to be taken to stop the bleeding. I advised her to use part of her next paycheck to pay her utilities and rent, and to cut up her two remaining credit cards. She did it in my office right then and there and agreed to use only cash from then on.

Then we turned to consider longer-term solutions. We talked about Maggie's skills and talents to see whether we could turn some of her creative juices into income. I discovered that Maggie often does the mounting and framing at the photographer's studio where she works. Maggie is very good at these tasks, so good that I encouraged her to call around and offer her services to others. This way, she'll have a second job, which will be a ladder for her to climb out of the well of debt she has stumbled into. Better still, it's a way for Maggie to add more value to her life and to regain the sense of control that spending and ballooning debt have stolen from her.

How can you add more value to your life? How can you rechannel your resources to make your energy and your money work for you?

Take a look at what happens when you suddenly get a $10,000 bonus or raise, or a $10,000 inheritance from a favorite grandparent, aunt, or uncle. Do you invest all or some of the money? If you don't, you're not alone, because not many people do. Some take that bundle and indulge in the dream vacation that's haunted them for years. Others add a wing to their house or buy a new home entertainment center. Unfortunately, none of these things will give you a cash flow in your future. But if you're like most people, you spread out the extra money over the year: You buy a nice Bordeaux or Barolo instead of the Gallo jug; you stop wearing L'eggs and start sporting Donna Karan; you go to more movies; you eat in nicer restaurants, and do it more often. Before the year ends, you've blown ten thousand bucks on a hundred small treats. You say, "I have no money. Where did it go?"

Once you get that extra income, bonus, raise, or inheritance, consider what importance you attach to it so that it can make a difference in your life. Here's an alternative to consider. See what happens if you splurge a mere $2,500 for a few bottles of nice wine, several new outfits, and a short holiday and invest the remaining $7,500 in a mutual fund—which is simply a basket of various stocks. At a conservative growth rate of 8 percent per year, you'll end up with $11,019.96 in only five years. Imagine your return if you find a faster-growing fund that pays you 12, 15, or 20 percent!

The quality of your life hasn't dramatically changed, but you've begun to ensure that you will be able to have the same life or a better one in the future. You've begun to run your life like a business, by earning a profit at the end of the year. You've started to "grow" money so that you don't have to do all the work yourself.

Making Your Mortgage Work for You

You can creatively grow money, too, by retooling how you allocate certain payments. Let me tell you another story. It's a good one with a happy ending. Once again, it happened during my visit to the Ranch.

I was out hiking with Betty Scott early one morning. She has a bum knee, so she had to pause for a brief rest. I was glad to stop so I could witness the sun's incredible orange rays, which were just beginning to pierce the purplish haze draped over those gorgeous Mexican mountains. We plunked ourselves down on a smooth rock, and Betty began talking to me about my work.

"I see you're no longer running Perry Investments but have

started this company called Take Charge Financial! I like the name. How does it fit?" she asked as we started up the trail once again.

"Well, we're developing really good strategies so we can help people create their financial futures, and we're changing the language so people can get it, employ it, and achieve measurable results," I said. "Just a small task," I added with a grin.

"That sounds really interesting. Can you give me an example of what you mean?" asked Betty, ever the lawyer.

"Sure. Listen, you bought a house a few months ago, right?"

"Yes. A gorgeous Victorian with lots of potential. I'm having the back porch remodeled as soon as I can handle the expenses."

"Give me details," I inquired, ever the financial counselor. "What's your mortgage, and for how long?"

"Thirty-year mortgage, $180,000," said Betty, as she sidestepped a huge gray boulder.

"Well, by the time your interest is paid, you'll be in your seventies, and that house will have cost you over half a million dollars. But if you pay the principal and the interest each month, *plus the principal of the following month's payment,* you'll cut your mortgage about half—in both time and dollars."

Betty turned to me and said, "Oh!" She was tumbling the information around in her brain.

We started up the last steep grade that leads to the "pig," a big granite rock formation that really looks like a pig. It was so welcome because seeing it meant that we were at the top of the long climb. We hikers always kiss the pig when we get to the top. From there it's a loop back to the Ranch, around the edge of those rock-ribbed mountains. We hiked in silence for a few minutes, drinking in the glorious morning air. Suddenly, Betty turned around and said enthusiastically, "I got it!"

Because my head was already off in another direction, I asked, "Well, what did you get?" The scenery—and the air—had put me in a pleasant daze.

"What I got, first of all, is that if I follow what you say about paying my mortgage, I'm going to own my house when I'm fifty-five or so, and not when I'm seventy or seventy-five, which is a huge difference. Second, I'm going to save about two hundred thousand dollars or more, which is a lot of money for my later years. I think I can do what you say. I'd rather benefit me than the bank! If I remember the way my mortgage works, it means initially paying only about eighty dollars more each month. I can definitely do that," she said, glowing.

Betty was right about how her monthly tab breaks down in terms of principal and interest. You can easily determine what your principal is by reading your statement. It should tell you how much you have paid toward interest and how much you have paid toward your principal. If your statement does not provide this information, then call your mortgage company or bank and find out.

You, too, can save a bundle by using this simple mortgage-repayment strategy—and retain money you'll need for your future.

PLANNING AHEAD

Since money can grow for you to meet your future needs, let's figure out just how much money you'll need when you reach the time that you'll want to be free from working for income. For most of us, that age is sixty-five or seventy.

Lately, however, an increasing number of Americans are easing out of working as young as thirty-five or forty. Why? As a *Wall Street Journal* article published August 21, 1996, said, these young "retirees" are responding to two contemporary phenomena: "New Age values" and a "robust stock market." They are lucky enough to have made their fortunes in the stock market when they were young—and now understand that time, friends, family, and love are commodities more precious than cash. They stop working to enjoy what matters most to them, and they are financially able to do so because of the commitment and skill they employed to plan for their financial futures. Some stop working altogether; some simply cut back and work part-time or do a little consulting or community service; others stroll the boulevards of their dreams.

Obviously, these early "retirees" are a fortunate few who began investing when they were young. But you, too, can work toward the same goal, regardless of your age. You might not be able to stop working at thirty-five or forty, but maybe you'll be able to stop at fifty, fifty-five, or sixty.

Consider this question: When you do leave the workforce, do you want to preserve your current lifestyle, or are you willing to live on less money and cut back on certain extras or simple pleasures? Culturally, we've all been led to believe that we have to spend money to be happy. But now we're taking back power by discovering what is truly important to us. For some people, it may be a simpler life, less encumbered with possessions. Does this notion appeal to you?

I asked Betty to envision her life ten, twenty, or thirty years from now.

"That's a toughie," she admitted. "Up until now I always thought I'd work because that's all I ever did. Now, though, I don't know. I don't think I want to be a workaholic, and I know I'd like to do some traveling, but I've never really thought beyond next month or next year."

Betty sat back on the sofa by the sun-splashed bay window of my office. My cats, Gizmo and Muggs, curled up around her. She was very relaxed—an unusual feeling, she confessed. A smile danced across her face. "You know something—I've never really discussed this with anyone before—but I've always wanted to do pottery. I have this picture of myself sitting outside, looking up at the mountains with a mound of wet clay in my hands, fashioning bowls and plates. Can you picture me, the big-time lawyer, living like that? But maybe I could someday. And here's another thought: I've also considered a change in order to become a mentor to inner-city high school and college-age girls who might desire a career in law."

I was happy that Betty was exploring new and creative highways in her life, and with my encouragement, she decided to take a few days to examine her current lifestyle and project what her needs might be in the future, especially if she modifies her life as a highly charged lawyer and becomes an artisan and a mentor. Will she want to change her lifestyle? If so, what are the financial implications of this choice?

THE "RULE OF 72"

Will you want to alter your lifestyle a few years from now?

Let's say you're now forty years old. You're single with an annual income of $35,000. Your closet holds clothes you adore, you eat out occasionally, go to the movies on weekends, go to concerts every now and then, and enjoy a vacation away from home once a year.

Or perhaps you're married with a joint income of $60,000. You and your husband go away to a country cottage on weekends, drive two cars, play tennis and golf, entertain friends, and travel each year.

Now, how much cash will you need in order to continue that lifestyle once you stop working? The temptation is to say, "A lot." But how much is a lot? And where is it going to come from? There's an old saying about how you find wealth: You can marry it, inherit it, or earn it. (Of course, you can also steal it—but stealing rarely works for long, and we're going to keep things honest here.)

Let's say the only wealth you have and are likely to have is what you earn. And with your $60,000 salary, you spend about $4,000 a month for mortgage payments or rent, car payments, clothes, food, entertainment, and credit cards. To maintain this lifestyle, you'll need to have invested $600,000 by the time you stop working so that at a (fairly typical) 10 percent rate of return, you and your husband can continue to receive the same income as you do now—$60,000 a year.

Similarly, with a yearly income of $35,000, you'll need to have invested $350,000 by the time you ease out of working in order to support your lifestyle.

Basically, then, you can add another zero to whatever you currently earn to determine a ballpark figure of how much you will need to have by the time you ease out of working so that you can maintain your present cash flow.

Of course, inflation changes that canvas. You won't know what the rate of inflation will be at the time you decide to stop working, but inflation has been running at an average rate of 3 percent per year for the past decade. A moderate inflation rate, like the one we've experienced over the past decade, will increase the amount of savings you will need by a greater or lesser extent, depending on how far into the future you plan to live on the cash flow from your investments.

Now, that $600,000 we just discussed might seem like a whole lot of money. But let me tell you about a second jewel for your financial treasure chest. This second gem is called the "**Rule of 72.**" It's a simple mathematical calculation to help you understand the growth of your money. Here's how it works. *Take whatever rate of return you expect to earn, and divide the number 72 by it to determine how many years it will take for your money to double at that rate.*

For example, let's say the rate of return you use is 12 percent, the average rate of return in the stock market. Divide 72 by 12. This equals 6. That means it will take six years for your money to double at that rate. Why use the stock market? Because it's the fastest and most proven way to double your money. In 1995—an exceptional year for the stock market—the market gave returns of 36 percent to investors, which means that at that rate, if you got this return in the stock market, your money would double in two years. A savings account at a bank currently averages 3 percent, and it would therefore take twenty-four years for your money to double. Underlying the Rule of 72, then, is the principle that a fair rate of return makes a significant difference in the growth of your money.

According to the Rule of 72, if you're forty years old, money you've invested now at an expected growth rate of 12 percent can double four times by the time you reach sixty-four. Thus, if you have already invested, for example, $40,000, it can double four times to $640,000 in twenty-four years. (It would grow to $80,000 at age forty-six, $160,000 at age fifty-two, $320,000 at age fifty-eight, and $640,000 at age sixty-four.) So, as you can see, if your investments are working for you, your money naturally grows so you can reach the $600,000 we talked about.

The Rule of 72 is a handy tool for forecasting the growth of your money and determining its future potential for you. And it exemplifies the power money can have for women. Who would want to miss the opportunity to put this resource to work in her life?

Let's take a look at Linette Atwood, my New York marketing friend who's struggling with a divorce, and find out how she finally used the principles of good money growth.

We met for lunch one day while I was in New York on business. I hadn't seen Linette since my visit to the Ranch. Her divorce was proceeding, and her lawyer had sorted through some of the financial muck that had so clouded her perceptions months before. In her professional guise, Linette looked much more in control, self-assured, and competent. You would never have guessed that this woman hadn't been in charge of her own financial life all along.

Over lunch, Linette told me that a "little voice" had been nudging her for a while to do something, but she'd been ignoring it.

"You know, Joan, I'm working on an account for a woman's magazine right now. I just might talk to the editor about doing a column about the illusions women create about their financial lives. Maybe that will get more people talking about it," Linette said. "I never talked about my money to anyone, ever. Frankly, with my friends, the subject never came up. But now that I'm in a crisis, it's on my mind all the time and I feel a little freer about opening up to the people closest to me."

Linette told me a little more about her life. She originally had gone to work so that she could have spending power, and she looked great in the latest fashions. But she hadn't moved on to the next priority—long-term financial growth. Now, with her life turned upside down by divorce, she needed to get her house in order. In particular, she needed to start saving and investing so that her daughter would be able to attend college in a few years.

Linette had stopped at a certain point in her maturity—taking control of your financial life is a maturation process. Her spending was not necessarily in line with her long-term financial objectives. How many clothes and stuff do we really need? Linette is seeing that, like some women, she's devoted herself to beautifying her body and her home without nurturing her soul. The outside looks like a million bucks; the inside is a house of cards. Developing a financial life, however, is about a state of mind. Being financially solvent isn't just about having money, but about having the temperament for managing your money.

"You do have options, Linette," I volunteered.

"Such as?"

"You can keep your present job, make the same salary, and dramatically cut your expenses, or you can creatively add to your income—either way, you'll increase your bottom line," I said.

I showed her the Earnings Outlook chart below. This chart shows, based on what she earns today, how much money goes through her hands.

EARNINGS OUTLOOK

Monthly Income	10 Years	20 Years	30 Years	40 Years
$1,000	$120,000	$240,000	$360,000	$480,000
$2,000	$240,000	$480,000	$720,000	$960,000
$3,000	$360,000	$720,000	$1,080,000	$1,440,000
$4,000	$480,000	$960,000	$1,440,000	$1,920,000
$5,000	$600,000	$1,200,000	$1,800,000	$2,400,000
$6,000	$720,000	$1,440,000	$2,160,000	$2,880,000
$7,000	$840,000	$1,680,000	$2,520,000	$3,360,000
$8,000	$960,000	$1,920,000	$2,880,000	$3,840,000
$9,000	$1,080,000	$2,160,000	$3,240,000	$4,320,000
$10,000	$1,200,000	$2,400,000	$3,600,000	$4,800,000

"I'll leave you with this thought: When you were married, you spent more than $10,000 a year on clothes, jewelry, vacations, and extras for your daughter, Kimberly, right?" Linette nodded. "Well, if you cut out most of that and save $7,500 to invest each year, you can grow that money so that you'll have an annual income of $100,000—less taxes and inflation adjustments—by the time you're age sixty-five. Just remember that little 'jewel' I'm always talking about: Spend less than you earn, invest the difference, then reinvest the returns."

Linette promised to give some thought to what I had said. If she takes control of her financial life by spending less each year and investing the difference, she will be able to live comfortably in the twenty-first century. She will enhance her life by approaching it this way. It's all a matter of learning how to selectively spend money. By reevaluating her priorities, she can set new goals for her money and be more self-assured in terms of how she spends. By engaging in the financial part of her Wheel of Life, she will give herself breathing room to work on her family problems and to bring the spiritual and mental parts of her Wheel into balance, too. She'll have peace of mind, knowing that she and her daughter will be in good shape for life. The ability of invested money to grow is the key to achieving this goal.

Are you convinced that making your money work for you, starting today, can make all the difference in your future? If so, it's time to take a closer look at your wealth-building options.

5

Your Money Machine:
Income for Life

The Money Machine

Dignity Money

Growing Toward Financial Freedom

t was several days before I heard back from Betty. When I saw her, she literally bounced into my office, with a sparkle in her eyes. My heart gladdened. This is the part I like best about working with any new person—the moment she has made a decision to take over her future financial life.

Betty beamed and waited for me to speak first. "Okay, I'm all ears. What is it?" I asked with a knowing smile.

"I got it! I really got it!" Betty bubbled. "I'm losing by not growing my money. Joan, I want to start planting right away."

Betty's power was about to be unleashed. I asked her how it felt.

"How does it feel? Like I'm in the middle of a revolution," she answered with a laugh. And she's right. We're all in the midst of a revolution.

I remember a discussion I had back in the 1970s about the Equal Rights Amendment. A large circle of professional women sat around a table in a Philadelphia restaurant talking adamantly about legislating our rights as women as a way to secure those rights. I argued that economic power was the key, and that legislating our rights wouldn't be the simple answer. I thought at that time—and I continue to think—that our strength rests in our ability to fortify our financial well-being and then to have the independence and courage to stand up for what we truly believe in our hearts. We have to make our stand regardless of what lawmakers do.

It's all part of the revolution, the last leg of the larger women's movement, which got lost in the "me first" shuffle of the 1980s and early 1990s. You must realize the enormity of this moment: You can actually own your financial future! You have the right to economic independence. This moment is as dramatic as when women won the right to vote, and is a monumental time in history—a period that has far-reaching implications for our lives and our world.

"So where do I go from here?" Betty wanted to know.

Betty, like so many professional women, was accustomed to being on top of things, to being in control, and to being capable of making decisions without batting an eye. All of a sudden, she was stymied. Devising financial strategies seemed as mystifying to Betty—whose idea of cooking was choosing from a take-out menu—as concocting the perfect béarnaise sauce. But her joyful spirit motivated her.

"No one starts out as an expert, Betty. We all begin from *somewhere* in every area of our lives—from school to career to relationships. The good news is that you already have strategies that are working for you in these other areas and that will help you be successful in the financial part of your life, too," I said.

"And in your financial life, you have the beginnings of an important concept I call the '**Money Machine.**' It's another of my secret 'jewels.' "

"The Money Machine! I like the sound of that," Betty said. "What exactly is it?"

"Your Money Machine is where you put your cash and let it grow. It is the generator of all the cash you'll need in order to lead a healthy, stress-free, and joyful life. Think of it as a pot of invested capital that is sufficient to create the returns that will meet your personal financial goals."

"Wow! That's sounds better than the Porsche I've been dreaming about. But how does it work? Please tell me more." Betty sat back to learn all about the Money Machine, my third financial jewel.

THE MONEY MACHINE

Think of your Money Machine as a well-oiled piece of equipment that churns and burns as it works for you, even when you don't. A properly tended Money Machine is a constant, reliable source of cash flow. If you nurture it correctly, you'll eventually reach a point in your life when your Money Machine takes over for you. When that happens, you no longer *have to* work. Instead, you'll work only because you love what you're doing. That's financial freedom!

The secret of creating a Money Machine is the "spend less than you earn and invest the difference" approach. Each month, you give part of your earnings to your Money Machine. You make sure to regularly feed your Money Machine before you "donate" cash to the nearest multiplex or restaurant or department store.

Betty liked that idea. Having her own Money Machine will allow her to stop working to support herself so that she can have time to pursue the things she loves. Back at the Ranch, she had talked about adding more value to society and to her own life by giving something back. More recently, when I asked Betty how she envisioned her life a few years from now, she talked about wanting to make pottery and to counsel young would-be lawyers. I could see her face glow as she talked about how these desires tap into her passion. She wants to welcome her creative and artistic side, and to become part of the bigger picture of improving society. But she never had a firm financial plan that would allow her to realize her dreams.

I suggested that life was too short for her to delay pursuing her passions, and that, possibly, she could find a way to begin to incorporate pottery and mentoring into her life right now.

Many of us can relate to Betty's dreams. Who wants to be a slave to money—to be held captive to a corporation, institution, or government agency by a paycheck? Most of us would pursue a variety of interests if money were not a factor. We each dream of a lifelong quest—to learn a new skill, to do volunteer work, to start a small business, or simply to have some free time to go out and have fun. With a well-running Money Machine, you can do it.

The Money Machine is designed to be a holding pen for cash that will be invested and doubled again and again until it's sufficient to generate the sum you will use to meet your monthly expenses throughout your life. Remember the Rule of 72: The incredible ability of money to grow works to your advantage, and it is the grease that makes your machine hum.

This is the purpose of your Money Machine—to let you walk away from having to go to work each day to earn income. Your Money Machine will assume the role of providing income to pay your living expenses. At this point, you will have arrived at financial freedom, and once you set up your Money Machine, you will have it for life.

Furthermore, the Money Machine allows you to serve your community at some point in your life. Part of being a well-balanced person—of having a smooth ride on your Wheel of Life—is not only enjoying personal benefits from your Money Machine, but also allocating some of those funds to good deeds. When we have ample financial resources, we can and must give back some to the society that has helped nurture us and supported our economic well-being. After all, everything we've gained in life has been a gift to us. Giving and sharing are also part of the power and joy of money.

Your Money Machine isn't a piggy bank designed simply to hold a bundle of cash. Nor is it the repository of one single investment. It is the sum of all your investments—the reservoir of capital wisely invested to yield solid, steady returns. Your Money Machine will be producing during the years when income is needed and wanted— and with a surprisingly low level of maintenance. With a well-tended Money Machine, you'll enjoy that good feeling in the pit of your stomach that comes from being able to say, "I've guaranteed my financial future, and I feel great about it."

Feeding Your Money Machine

Of course, you won't want to take your Money Machine for granted. As in other areas of your life, if you don't contribute, you don't get anything back. Try having a relationship in which all you do is take. Or try having a job where you do nothing but expect to be paid. Neither one will last very long. In the same way, your Money Machine depends upon your being a giver, not a taker. I'm talking about being not just a one-time contributor, or an on-again, off-again, sort-of contributor, but a consistent contributor. I'm talking about making the Money Machine a priority in your life. Because, by looking out for your financial future, you're also caring for your soul. Remember the Wheel of Life, and you'll realize that you must nurture and inspire all seven areas of your being.

When you feed your Money Machine, you can't dump just any old investment into it. Imagine someone with terrible eating habits, who puts lots of fats and sugars into his or her body. Over time, this person loses energy, slows down, and may even become ill because his or her body is not properly fueled. Your Money Machine is like your body: You can't put garbage into it and expect a healthy return. What are the "fats" and "sugars" of the investment world? There are two kinds of unhealthy investments to avoid: (1) investments that are excessively risky—investments in which you could lose all of your money—and (2) investments that have an inadequate rate of growth—investments that simply won't pay you very much.

In the next few chapters, we'll talk about your investment choices. I'll explain how to pick investments that will grow at a healthy rate without unnecessary risks and how to pick investments with tax advantages, which can boost your return even further. The food you feed to your Money Machine will determine the quality of your future.

The creation of a Money Machine begins with your first investment, and with the plan you devise to add to it regularly. It is not something that can solve your financial problems all at once, like winning the lottery. It's a process. It might take ten, fifteen, or twenty years to fully fund your machine, depending on how much and how often you contribute to it, when you first begin, and how wisely you select your investments.

When you decide to build your Money Machine, you embark on a voyage toward financial freedom. You'll definitely choose to get on with this journey.

DIGNITY MONEY

You'll rev up your Money Machine by first creating what I call "dignity money." This is money you'll need down the road in order to live a very minimal, luxury-free life. It's your insurance, so to speak, against destitution. You can figure out how much dignity money you'll need by determining the smallest amount that it will cost you to live each month. Using the Dignity Money worksheet on the next page, add up what you spend each month for food, transportation, taxes, housing, telephone, utilities and insurance. Don't include any frills. The monthly expense for dignity money will most likely be less than what you calculated on the Lifestyle Expenses worksheet on page 90. Remember, that worksheet included the extras—vacations, dinners out, clothing, electronic equipment, entertaining, and so on. Now we're examining the basics.

One very important basic is your home. If you own your house or apartment, your mortgage or maintenance is likely to be one of your major expenses; it is perhaps your single greatest expense. Paying off your mortgage greatly reduces your monthly outlay and therefore reduces your total dignity-money requirement. For many women, eliminating mortgage debt is an essential step to achieving financial independence.

Calculate your dignity-money needs both ways—with a mortgage and without. Depending on the current size and condition of your Money Machine, you may find that financial independence may arrive for you only after the mortgage is paid, whether that date is five, ten, or more years from now. Of course, the sooner the better!

DIGNITY MONEY

Monthly Expenses	*Minimum Amount*
Food	$_____
Housing	$_____
Telephone	$_____
Utilities	$_____
Transportation	$_____
Insurance	$_____
Total dignity money	
Total monthly expense	$_____
Total yearly dignity money	$_____
(equals total monthly expense × 12)	
Money machine target	
to create dignity money	$_____
(equals total yearly dignity money × 10)	

Your dignity-money calculation can be a rough number; that's okay. It might be $1,000 a month or $10,000. Each person's sum will be different. In any event, your dignity-money figure is the target level of income for the first stage of your Money Machine. Your goal is to generate this amount of cash from your Money Machine each month so you won't have anxiety about the basic care of yourself in the future.

If you already have your dignity money, then you can feel at ease. Knowing that you're financially secure should give you a good feeling all over and relieve whatever stressful flutters you might have had. If you have yet to establish your dignity money, then it's time to begin working toward it. Believe me, no outing, new trinket, or other toy is worth the cost of not taking this step.

Figuring Out Your Dignity Money

How do you figure out how much your Money Machine needs in order to generate your dignity money? The calculation is simple. Multiply your monthly dignity money by 12; then add a 0. This provides an estimate of how much money you'll need to invest in order to generate the appropriate monthly income.

For example, if your minimal monthly expenses are $4,000, then multiply $4,000 by 12 and add a 0. That means your yearly expenses will total $48,000. Your Money Machine will need $480,000 in order to provide you with dignity money. Why? At $4,000 a month, your yearly expenses will total $48,000. The rate of return on investments varies, of course, but history shows that a conservatively well-tended Money Machine should yield approximately 10 percent each year. This means that your Money Machine will need $480,000 in order to pay you an annual income at the rate of 10 percent per year, or $48,000.

The same formula—monthly expenses times 12, plus a 0—works for any expense level. If your minimal monthly expenses are $6,000, your Money Machine should contain $720,000: $6,000 times 12 is $72,000; adding a 0 brings it to $720,000. If your monthly expenses are $1,500, then you'll need $180,000 in your Money Machine. Do your own calculation.

This calculation requires one important adjustment—deductions based on the inflation rate. Inflation gradually shrinks your money's value. Therefore, whatever figure you compute will be worth less in the future. Consequently, the amount in your Money Machine will have to be somewhat greater to compensate for the effects of inflation.

Unfortunately, no one can know for sure how high the inflation rate will be in the future. A high inflation rate, like the one we experienced in the 1970s, will have a strongly negative effect on the value of the money generated by your Money Machine. The moderate inflation we've had so far during the 1990s (averaging around 3 percent a year) isn't nearly so powerful. Use the "Rule of 72" in reverse to estimate the effect of inflation on your Money Machine requirements: If you divide the inflation rate of 3 into 72, your dollar will be worth half as much in 26 years. This will be close to how much you will need in your Money Machine in order to generate a basic income.

The power of inflation grows significantly as time passes. If you are only one or two years away from the time when you plan to ease out of working, inflation will have little effect on your plans. But if you expect to work for two or three more decades, inflation will make a noticeable difference. For example, over twenty-four years, a modest 3 percent inflation rate per year will greatly increase how much dignity money you'll need. So the $2,000 a month you now spend for basic expenses might rise to $3,000 or more by the time you stop working. In addition, whether income withdrawn from your Money Machine is taxable or not is a significant factor. We'll discuss in a later chapter the effect of taxes on your money strategies. For now, just make a mental note that taxes will affect your financial plans, and let's continue working with your rough dignity-money calculation.

Let's say you calculate your dignity money to be a whopping $600,000. That seems like a lot of money to feed to your Money Machine, and the thought of how to amass such an amount might be daunting. But if you save this $600,000 gradually, rather than all at once, it will be much less intimidating.

Consider Rachel Levine. Remember Rachel? She's the assistant museum curator who lives with her husband in a house they're fixing up in Dallas. Rachel earns $30,000 a year. When I met her, with her discreet diamond earrings and self-assured air, I imagined that Rachel had already begun to build a financial future for herself. I was wrong. Once we warmed to each other in the hot tub at the Ranch, she easily confessed that her fiscal future was tottering a bit and asked what she could do at her age, starting with the $10,000 she and her husband had squirreled away in money market funds.

Rachel and I chatted about the dignity-money concept, and she concluded that she and her husband would want to have $600,000 in their Money Machine. Here's a closer look at how Rachel and David can accumulate the dignity money they'll be looking for in later years.

Rachel enjoys museum work, and David enjoys his work, too. So they see themselves working into their mid-sixties. That's about thirty-six years from today. Using the Rule of 72, we calculate that if their money grows at an average annual rate of 10 percent (a conservative average return on stocks), it will double every 7.2 years. In thirty-six years, when they reach sixty-six, their current $10,000 investment can double five times:

$$\$10,000 \times 2 = \$20,000$$

$$\$20,000 \times 2 = \$40,000$$

$$\$40,000 \times 2 = \$80,000$$

$$\$80,000 \times 2 = \$160,000$$

$$\$160,000 \times 2 = \$320,000 \text{ at age } 66$$

So with their current savings of $10,000 alone, they're halfway to their goal! Now all they need to do is squirrel away some money each month in order to meet the other half of their goal. It is likely Rachel's income will increase with raises, promotions, and career moves, and David's contracting business is expanding rapidly. This should dramatically raise his annual profits. As the Levines eventually accumulate more cash to invest, their Money Machine will gain more steam. Another plus: They have only about $50,000 left to pay on their mortgage, so they will own their house by the time they want to ease out of working full-time.

To grow my own dignity money, I estimate that I will probably need to put $700,000 in my Money Machine. That means I'll have $70,000 a year to live on. To advance to the next step—to live more freely, to travel several times a year, and to entertain and frolic without guilt at some of my favorite stores—in other words, to maintain my present lifestyle—I will have to have more cash invested in my Money Machine. I will need in excess of $1 million. And to dream bigger, I'll require several million dollars. The important thing to note is that creating the Money Machine begins with securing your financial necessities and then moving on. And the tools are at hand to make this process easier than our fears would lead us to believe.

Betty figures she'll need less dignity money than I do. She earns $76,000 a year as an attorney at a small public-interest firm that specializes in environmental law. Betty grasps the principle of spending less than you earn and investing the difference and is prepared to do exactly that. Right now, her basic, no-frills monthly expenses total $3,500. That means her Money Machine will have to contain $420,000 to establish her dignity money.

"If I cut back my expenses, I think I can eventually squeeze out $10,000 to invest," Betty announced.

"That means you have to really shave those credit cards," I reminded her.

But if Betty is able to commit $10,000 a year to her Money Machine, she'll be in great shape by the time she's sixty-five. If she were to invest that cash in a private pension plan (known as a flexible premium variable life insurance plan)—which will be discussed fully in Chapter 8—she could enjoy $89,600 of tax-free income, from a 12 percent return, from the time she reaches sixty-five to age eighty-five. Sounds good, huh? I'll show you how to do this, too. The benefits of securing tax-free income from your Money Machine are pretty obvious.

"It's that simple?" Betty asked.

"Yes. It can be simple and very doable," I replied. "There is no reason to develop indigestion pondering what your financial picture will be in the future. It's possible to handle it all along the way and still have a good time enjoying life as you go."

"And what do I have to do with my Money Machine in the meantime? What's the maintenance?" Betty hurled a chain of questions; this is exactly what you *should* do when devising wealth-building strategies and growing and maintaining your Money

Machine. Ask as many questions as you wish in order to feel comfortable. Then take action.

"I have a house. Does that count in my Money Machine?" Betty asked.

Many people I talk to say that they have a big investment in their house, and they count this as an asset for the future. But remember, your house is money in "jail." The same is true for your car. That's because these two commodities have your money tied up, unable to work for you.

Your house and your car exist mostly for your use: They don't produce cash flow to meet your expenses. That's why they're not in your Money Machine. There are exceptions: If you rent a room in your house and collect rent, it's a cash-producing asset. And, of course, commercial real estate is a definite investment option. But under normal circumstances, not only do your house and your car not produce income, but they usually require upkeep, which raises your monthly expenses.

Similarly, I'm sometimes asked whether a small business you own is part of your Money Machine. No, not if you *are* the business—that is, if your labor is central to making it work. When that's the case, annual profits from your business are much like your salary from a job: This is work income that you'd like to eventually replace with investment income so that you have the option of walking away from work when you're ready to do so. For your business to be an investment in your Money Machine, it has to have value independent of your labor and thus, the potential to be sold to someone else for cash.

If you want to turn a small business into a Money Machine investment, you, as the entrepreneur, may have to change roles. You must stop being the center of your business and begin shaping it so that it can exist without you. Think of your business as you would a child: It has to grow up and leave home. Only then will your business be an asset in your Money Machine.

GROWING TOWARD
FINANCIAL FREEDOM

Your Money Machine houses all of your investments, including brokerage accounts, company-sponsored retirement plans, private pension plans, real estate, and other investments that generate cash. You made a list of your income-producing assets on page 92. You'll learn more about how to choose investments for your Money Machine in the next few chapters. For now, the key point is this: The time to begin growing your Money Machine is today.

Where will you be in a decade or more? What resources do you need and desire for your future years? Have you ever noticed that when you take the time to create a plan, opportunities and tools for realizing that plan seem to present themselves? Our creativity kicks into gear, and we tap inner resources we never imagined existed. This happens in our money life as well: When you begin thinking about what your Money Machine can do to support you, all sorts of things might come to help you. But first, trust in the process. And second, create some motion.

Let's take a look at a few women who are in various stages of gearing up.

First there's Patricia, Maggie O'Neal's mother. As confused and daunting as Maggie's financial picture is, Patricia's is an even greater challenge. Patricia is fifty years old and earns $50,000 a year as a senior publicist for a movie studio. But she has no savings, no outside income, and no investments.

When I met Patricia, I asked her to think about her relationship with money and how her beliefs were responsible for creating her life. As we talked, it became clear that Patricia's money attitudes have held her back throughout her life. Her father was a political science professor who held strong socialist beliefs; her mother was a dance instructor who had spent time in the artistic quarters of New York's Greenwich Village. When Patricia was growing up, her parents' words and actions gave her the false belief that wanting money was somehow "greedy," that living a bohemian lifestyle and eschew-

ing investment, saving, and other activities associated with capital-
ism were better.

I asked her to question whether her deep-seated beliefs about
money were helping her to enjoy success and security. If she found
that some weren't, I suggested that she use the "delete" key, just like
the one on a computer keyboard, to wipe those negative messages
off the screen. Being stuck in backward thinking was not going to
work for her financial future.

Patricia is divorced. She lives in a low-rent apartment in New
York City. As we've seen, she often gives Maggie money to see Maggie through, even if it means sacrificing her own desires. Aside from
the task of rearranging her belief system concerning money, she
faces a major challenge because she doesn't own anything in her
Money Machine, and her working time frame is not a long one. Patricia needs to make a quick mental shift and go for it. Either she
has to find another job that pays more, or she really has to commit
to the "spend less than you earn and invest the difference" strategy.
At Patricia's age, she will have to make a deeply serious commitment. And she'll have to cut out her stream of handouts to Maggie—for Maggie's sake as well as her own.

Having pondered these realities, Patricia has determined that she
can scrape together $10,000 for an initial investment. In Chapter 9,
you'll see how, with a $10,000-a-year contribution, Patricia could
end up with $31,815 of tax-free income each year for twenty years,
beginning at age sixty-five. If she works until she's seventy—which
is a likelihood—she could be set up with an annual income of
$58,369 for twenty years from her Money Machine. In either case,
this tax-free income will nicely augment the pension she'll receive
from her job at the film studio, where she first started working
when she was twenty-three.

One thing is certain: Some income is better than no income, and
despite her age, Patricia has a window of opportunity. She has some
high hurdles to clear, but she's on her way to taking charge of her financial future. She's beginning to understand the power of money
and her power to make money work for her.

Like Patricia, Betty is committed to investing $10,000 a year. She can get more gusto out of her options than Patricia because she is eight years younger. Betty's private pension plan (flexible premium variable life insurance) will generate $89,600 each year beginning when she's sixty-five and continuing until she's eighty-five. This story illustrates the difference between investing now and waiting to invest later. Think of the game of golf and the rapid growth that's possible when money has time to multiply. Betty gets to benefit from the upward curve of the growth of money because she's taking action earlier in her life than Patricia. As a result, she'll reach a point in her life when she no longer must work but chooses to because she loves doing what she's doing. Patricia may have to wait longer than Betty to enjoy that option.

Now, if you really want to see what a dramatic difference age makes when you're growing wealth, just remember Rachel's story. As you may recall, she began investing when she was in her late twenties. At thirty years old, she's still young, so there's plenty of time for her money to grow. She and David have the opportunity to build a Money Machine that is capable of generating significantly greater income than they require to support their needs. As a result, they'll be able to make charitable contributions so they can make other people happy, too. And Rachel plans to use part of the funds in her Money Machine to eventually pay for the education of the child they anticipate having.

Rachel and David decided they needed some discipline, so they signed up for automatic withdrawal: Their bank will automatically withdraw money from each of their checking accounts every month and contribute this money to their Money Machine. This way, they will never miss a chance to invest. Now they're off and running. In time, they will have the option to stop working and enjoy the proceeds of their Money Machine.

Finally, there's Maggie. Remember, she's been living from paycheck to paycheck, accumulating more and more credit card debt and trying to keep one step ahead of total financial ruin. What can she do?

The first step for Maggie is to peel away the layer of hopelessness that's preventing her from making any positive moves. Then she'll make a strong commitment to herself: If she pays attention to the "first secret jewel," she will probably find that she can save from $50 to $100 a month from her annual salary of $18,000 and any extra income she might get from odd jobs here and there. A hundred dollars a month in a money market account (housed in a new Plus IRA, which will be discussed in Chapter 9) can accumulate and build enough cash for Maggie to invest in a mutual fund or stock. She'll be surprised how much her money will add up. Later, if she moves on to a higher-paying job, she will be in the habit of regularly investing in her Money Machine. At twenty-five, she's in great shape to watch her money grow—if she starts now.

All of us, one way or another, will eventually be looking to our Money Machines to maintain and enhance the quality of our lives. Trust that you have the talent, the tools, the knowledge, and the resources to start your Money Machine and to build it into a potent force to enrich your spirit. Go for it!

6

The Three
File Cabinets:
Library of Investments

How Do You Want to Be Taxed?

───────────────

C heck this out," I said to Betty. I motioned to a picture on my desk of three file cabinets. In the drawing, each file cabinet has the same three drawers, labeled stocks, bonds, and real estate.

"This drawing represents the choices you can make to fill your Money Machine with healthy investments. It's a tool that allows you to visualize the organization of your financial life."

Betty quickly scanned the sketch, which will be her reference for the choices she'll have as she decides what works best for her. The drawers of each file cabinet contain the types of investments—stocks, bonds, and real estate—from which you can choose, while the three file cabinets show the three different ways you can be taxed.

The sketch has two distinctive features. First, notice that the drawers in the file cabinets are the same: stocks, bonds, real estate.

These represent the only viable alternatives you have for investing your cash in order to build your Money Machine: stocks, bonds, real estate. They don't include investment oddities, like commodities, futures, precious metals, or "collectible items," like antiques, rare coins, or art. Stocks, bonds, and real estate are the sum of your real choices.

I've omitted the investment oddities for good reason. Commodities and futures are highly complex investment vehicles with their own specialized markets and a wealth of arcane theories about how to invest in them. Unless you intend to become an expert in these investments—which is a full-time job in itself—you'll be steering clear of them. Similarly, you won't invest long-term money in collectible items, like art, coin collections, rare books, or antique automobiles, unless you have a deep personal interest in them. Paintings, for example, are wonderful to look at, but they aren't dependable investments for your Money Machine; the value of paintings rises and falls unpredictably as fads sweep the art world, and the hot artist whose work skyrockets in price this year is likely to plummet in reputation next year. You won't want to hang your dignity money on fads!

Keep it simple. Stick to stocks, bonds, and real estate—all of which are bought and sold publicly in markets that regularly determine their value. That's why they are key choices for your Money Machine.

HOW DO YOU WANT TO BE TAXED?

The three file cabinets in the sketch illustrate your choices for how you'll want the federal government to tax your income and your investments. Uncle Sam drops in to collect his tax three times:

1. When you earn income from salary or business profits;
2. When your investments pay you dividends or interest; and
3. When you sell your investments and receive the profits.

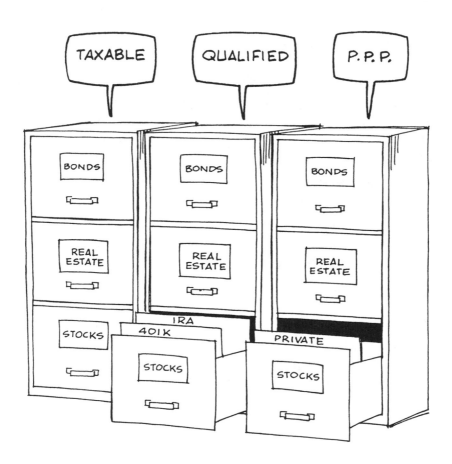

When to pay Uncle Sam and how much you'll have to give him are big factors in determining the income that your Money Machine will produce for your future. When you ease out of working and begin receiving cash from your Money Machine, will it come to you as taxable income, tax-free income, or a combination of both? If you have to pay tax on some of those funds, what will the tax rate be at that time in your life? And based on your understanding of the current economic and political climate, do you believe that taxes are going to rise or fall? These are important questions to consider, because the answers will help determine how much cash you'll be able to spend from your Money Machine later in your life.

If you have investments in **File Cabinet No. 1** (taxable investments), Uncle Sam taps on your door three times looking for tax dollars: when you earn money, when your investments pay you dividends or interest, and when you sell your investments and make a profit.

For example, let's say you're planning to buy a piece of rental property with no special tax advantages—perhaps a small college-town apartment house, which you plan to rent out as student housing. This investment fits in the real estate drawer of File Cabinet No. 1. You'll purchase the property with after-tax dollars (money that has already been taxed at the time you earned it). As you profit from the rents the students pay you, the government will take a piece of the action. And if you sell the property and make a profit, Uncle Sam will be back for more tax. That last profit is a "capital gain"—the difference between the purchase price of your investment and the price when you sell it. So the money you invest in the rental property and the money you make from owning it will be taxed three separate times by the government.

In File Cabinet No. 1, the same is also true for a share of stock: You buy it with after-tax dollars, pay tax on dividends that you may receive while you own the stock, and pay tax on your capital gain when you sell the stock for more money than you paid for it. In other words, you're taxed across the board.

In **File Cabinet No. 2** (tax-deferred investments), Uncle Sam takes a different approach—a kinder, gentler one. He visits only once for tax collection. This file cabinet represents any type of investment that is known as a "qualified plan": traditional individual retirement accounts (IRAs), simplified employee pensions (SEP-IRAs), simple IRAs (employer-sponsored IRAs), Keogh plans, 401(k) plans, 403(b) plans, and company pension plans. Don't be thrown by the alphabet soup. The important thing to know is that you are taxed the same way on all of these investments.

Let's use a traditional IRA as an example. When you contribute, say, $2,000 to an IRA, you don't have to pay income tax on that money—you get a deduction from your taxable income on your income-tax return for that year. As the investments in your IRA grow, you don't pay any tax on their earnings. But when you withdraw money from your IRA—or any other qualified plan—Uncle Sam will be waiting for you. You will be taxed at the ordinary income-tax rate as you withdraw money.

In **File Cabinet No. 3** (tax-free investments), Uncle Sam takes yet another approach. This time, however, he is perhaps on his best behavior. Again, he shows up only once. You do pay tax on money you are investing—but it grows tax free. More significant, you're able to withdraw cash tax free down the road.

File Cabinet No. 3 is known as the flexible premium variable life insurance plan. But don't be put off by its name—you'll want to know about this type of investment. For our convenience, we'll call it the "private pension plan." By including variable term insurance with your mutual funds, you obtain certain benefits that, under the insurance law, include no tax on the growth or use of your money. This way Uncle Sam is *not* your partner when you're seventysomething, as he is with traditional IRAs and 401(k) plans.

The 1997 tax law revisions made provision for a new form of IRA: the so-called Roth IRA (also known as the American Dream IRA and the Plus IRA), which took effect in 1998. It allows you to contribute up to $2,000 a year in your IRA. Under the new legislation, you won't have a tax deduction for your contributions but you will be able to withdraw your funds tax free. If you earn over $95,000 a year or if you and your spouse jointly earn over $150,000, you can't use this IRA and, in any event, you're restricted to a $2,000 contribution per year. Although this new IRA is useful, it's not sufficient for most people to build a thriving Money Machine.

The new legislation also provided for an Education IRA whereby you can contribute $500 a year for a child until age eighteen. When the child reaches age thirty, the Education IRA converts to a Plus IRA.

Finally, under the new tax-law provisions, you can withdraw money from your traditional IRA before age fifty-nine and a half for only two purposes without incurring a penalty—for education and for first-time home buying.

The file-cabinet picture is a simple and accessible way for you to see where the investments in your Money Machine fit into your financial picture. If you have cash in a bank or money market account, think of it as being in a "To Be Filed" basket alongside the three file cabinets. That's because a money market account is a glorified savings account with low interest rates and it is not an investment to serve you as a productive wealth builder. It's money that's waiting for a place to go. If your company or employer provides an IRA or a 401(k) plan or if you have an IRA on your own, it's in File Cabinet No. 2. And I know you're wondering about File Cabinet No. 3, because the private pension plan is a newly talked about, but important, strategy for growing money these days.

Time and energy are the real premiums of our lives. Once your investments are neatly arranged in the drawers, you can see what investments will produce taxable or tax-free income, and you can apply the Rule of 72 to see how those investments will prosper. Finally, you'll be able to estimate your cash flow from your Money Machine.

Now that you have an overview, we'll examine each file cabinet more fully. In my own Money Machine, I've used all of the file cabinets and many of the drawers, depending upon my goals. You'll see how this works, too.

But first, let's open the three different drawers in each file cabinet and discuss what's inside. We'll start with the most important drawer—the stock drawer.

7

The Best
Investment Choices:
Stocks and Mutual Funds

The Stock Drawer
Riding the Investment Waves
Picking a Stock
Choosing a Mutual Fund

THE STOCK DRAWER

*H*istorically, stocks have outperformed all other investments, including bonds and real estate. So the stock drawer is a must for a thriving Money Machine. The stock drawer includes individual stocks and mutual funds, which are composed of various stocks. (More about those later.)

What is a stock? It represents a share of ownership in a company. Normally, a stock is traded on one of the following exchanges: the New York Stock Exchange (NYSE), the American Stock Exchange (ASE), the National Association of Securities Dealers Automated Quotations system (NASDAQ), the Pacific Stock Exchange (PSE), or the over-the-counter market (OTC). (You can tell when a stock is traded on the OTC, because it is listed by a symbol with four characters. For example, Apple, the computer company, on the OTC, has the symbol APPL, whereas IBM, which is traded on the New York Stock Exchange, has the symbol IBM.)

These various exchanges are like fraternities: Some guys decide to sign up with one, while others decide to sign up with another. If a stock is traded on an exchange, it means it must abide by the exchange's rules of public disclosure of information and generally accepted accounting guidelines.

Since a share of stock represents part ownership of a company, the prices of stock shares rise and fall depending on the earnings picture for the company. In *The Wall Street Journal, The New York Times,* or your local newspaper, stocks and their current prices are listed by initials or by combined parts of their names—not by their formal trading symbols. If you already know the abbreviation or listing name of your stock or mutual fund, it's merely a matter of looking it up. If you don't know the abbreviation, it's not too difficult to figure it out. For example, General Electric is listed as GenEl and Home Depot is listed as HmeDep.

In the newspaper, quoted prices are from the preceding day's trade, but the listing will also give you the stock's high and low prices over the past fifty-two weeks; the high and low prices for the day's trade; the dividend yield (that is, profits paid out to investors); the number of shares sold that day; and the P/E ratio, which is the price of a stock divided by the company's profits or earnings per share. A stock's P/E ratio is an important measure of how much investors are willing to pay for a dollar of a particular company's earnings, and is thus a strong indicator of the stock's currently perceived value—its popularity among investors.

As an example, let's look at General Electric. On November 7, 1996, GE closed at $102^3/4$, up by $1^1/8$ over the previous day's trade. Its high during November 7 was $103^1/8$, and its low was $100^7/8$. GE's dividend yield was 1.84 per share on that day, and its P/E was 24. The fifty-two-week high and low: $101^5/8$ and $62^1/8$. We can see that the price of GE stock is on the rise. It closed on November 7 at a price higher than any it had attained throughout the previous year.

Mutual funds, which are baskets of from twenty to fifty stocks or more, are also priced daily at the close of the day. You can look up their prices in financial papers or your local newspaper. Listings for mutual funds give slightly different information. The listing will tell you the net asset value (NAV) of the mutual fund's shares. The NAV is the combined daily price of all the stocks in the mutual fund's portfolio, as well as the year-to-date total return and the net change from the day before. Like individual stocks, mutual funds are also abbreviated. GT Global's Health Care mutual fund, for example, is listed under the GT Global fund family as HltCr.

There are lots of buyers and sellers of stocks on the various exchanges, which establish the daily pricing for each stock. The sizable mutual funds also have many buyers and sellers. The most important reason to buy a stock or a mutual fund for your Money Machine is the expectation that its price will rise. And the key factor in whether the price of a stock will rise is whether the company in which you own a share will make more money—more money this year than it did the last and more money next year. If this happens, the price of your stock will probably rise. As the company becomes more valuable, the value of your share of the company increases.

Let's look at Microsoft, the famous software company, for example. Its stock price has increased steadily, and has not only made Bill Gates a billionaire but created other happy millionaires. All of this has happened because the company and its employees are so adept at developing and marketing products that people are eager to buy. In January 1992, Microsoft stock sold for $20 a share. In November 1996, it was up to $140 a share. It took a dip between December 1995 through the first quarter of 1996, but then resumed its steady, awesome climb.

More than 80 percent of the personal computers in the world use Microsoft software, and the company was banking on its hold on the market when it launched its $150 million marketing campaign for Windows 95, the latest version of its most important program. Thanks to Microsoft's canny salesmanship, millions of people decided they "needed" this software for their computers (translation: they wanted to have it at once). People began lining up early in the morning at computer stores throughout the United States. Supplies ran out quickly, and some smaller stores had waiting lists. This indicated that Microsoft's profits were rising and that the stock price would continue to climb. By successfully expanding its revenue base, the company became even more valuable to its shareholders. This scenario is going on every day in the stock market.

Ultimately, the value of a stock depends on smart management of a company. If the managers develop great products or services and sell them brilliantly, as Microsoft does, the company's shares will grow in value. If they produce poor products or fail to build their markets for whatever reason—like being overtaken by the competition—the value of the company's shares will likely fall.

Mutual Funds: Collections of Stocks

A mutual fund is a collection of stocks chosen by a fund manager who has developed a skill at buying and selling stocks. Mutual funds allow you to invest in the stock market without having to make individual buy-and-sell decisions; the fund manager does that for you.

Mutual funds are the best way for a beginning investor to tap into the opportunities offered by the stock market. Here's why. Too many people invest in a stock solely because it was recommended by someone else. As a result, they often lose their investment. Many quit the stock market because of that one negative experience. By giving up, however, they miss an opportunity to grow their money. With a mutual fund investment, you'll be more secure. After all, the fund is composed of many stocks that each perform differently. Some of the stocks will do better than others, but overall, the fund's objective is to increase in value and grow your investment. So investing in a good mutual fund is a solid opportunity to broaden your investment prospects and to benefit from the market performance of various companies. This opportunity to invest in many stocks, not just one, diversifies the dollars that you invest and is one of the major advantages of mutual funds.

Many people choose to be in mutual funds because they're not interested in mastering the nuances of trading—the buying and selling of stocks. In this fashion, they don't actively manage their stock portfolios; they leave monitoring tasks to the mutual fund manager. The fund manager keeps a watchful eye on the appropriateness of stocks in the fund. So mutual funds are custom designed for investors who have little time and energy—and, perhaps, inclination—to constantly make quick buy-and-sell decisions.

Many mutual funds are part of "fund families" run by large investment companies. Fund families offer different types of funds for investors with different objectives and interests. You've probably heard of some of the largest mutual fund families, like Fidelity and Vanguard. A fund family can be composed of anywhere from two to two hundred funds. The GT Global family, for example, contains not only the Health Care fund but also the Consumer Products (ConsProd) fund, the Natural Resources (NatRes) fund, and the Telecommunications (Telcom) fund. If you have enough money, you can buy more than one mutual fund—for example, you can buy fund shares in both the Consumer Products and the Natural Resources funds—and thus further diversify your investments.

Some types of funds have historically performed better than others. Mutual funds composed of smaller companies that are poised to grow into much bigger companies generally outperform mutual funds composed of large, established corporations. These small-company funds are known as "small capitalization," or "small cap," funds and typically represent companies that are energetically developing new technologies. These would have included the microchip manufacturers and software developers of the 1970s. There usually will be more volatility in the price of a small cap fund than in the price of a fund composed of larger, established companies because the small caps are youngsters growing up.

By contrast, the "value" funds—often composed mainly of "large capitalization," or "large cap," stocks—typically include larger, established companies that are mature, like General Motors, Procter & Gamble, and AT&T. These companies have proven, established markets, but their stock value generally rises more slowly than that of successful, smaller, upstart firms. Value funds include medium and large companies that the fund manager believes are "values"— that is, bargains—because their shares are priced low in the market.

If the small cap funds have been the best performers among mutual funds, the "international" funds—those composed of companies represented on worldwide, not just American, stock markets—have been the second best. I'll talk more about the international marketplace for stocks and mutual funds elsewhere.

When you're selecting a mutual fund, ask to see what kind of stocks and what particular companies are in its portfolio so you can get a feel for the fund's objective and the stock-picking style of its manager. (Ask for a prospectus, a document that includes this information.) This will allow you to discover what themes or trends determine the composition of the fund and what types of industries go into consumer products, cyclical goods, technology. Is the fund composed of stocks of industries that specialize in health care or something else? For example, a technology fund might include Microsoft, Compaq, Intel, IBM, and other technology-driven stocks.

The Dow Jones Industrial Average

When I entered the financial industry in 1975, the Dow Jones Industrial Average, widely known as the "Dow," was hovering around the 800 mark. Today, it tops 8,000 and continues upward. Now, what do these numbers mean? The Dow is a way to measure the growth of the price of stocks in the United States by examining the prices of the same thirty industrial stocks each day. The Dow plots the rise and fall of these stocks as they are bought and sold, using them as a mirror of the stock market. It is a weather vane of sorts, as it heralds the ups and downs of Wall Street.

The Dow, which celebrated its centennial in 1996, has an interesting history. It was the brainchild of Charles Henry Dow, a newspaperman who founded a financial news service with another reporter, Edward Jones. The two men issued a newsletter called the *Customers' Afternoon Letter,* which began recording the average price for nine railroad and two industrial stocks in 1884. Then, on July 8, 1889, Dow Jones & Company started *The Wall Street Journal,* which is still the preeminent business newspaper in the United States.

Dow continued to hone his stock index, and in 1896 he finally launched the first of what we know as the Dow Jones averages. The first one measured a dozen stocks, including U.S. Leather, American Sugar, American Tobacco, Chicago Gas, and General Electric. Of the twelve original stocks, only General Electric remains on the index today. The other companies that were on the original Dow have closed, merged with others, or lost their place on the index as their importance in the U.S. economy diminished. The current makeup of the Dow reflects the changing American society: Disney, American Express, IBM, McDonald's, and Eastman Kodak are among the stocks listed now.

The Dow reached its first milestone in 1906, when it closed above 100 points. It continued its steady rise over the years. On October 28, 1929, the Dow took its deepest plunge. It fell 38.33 points, closing at 260.64. This was the great 1929 crash and the beginning of the Depression. The Dow didn't reach 500 until 1956. It exceeded 1,000 in 1972. Since then, it's had several dips, but it has always recovered to rise higher than before.

There are other indexes of stock market growth, some of which are probably more accurate barometers. For example, the Standard & Poor's 500 Index (often simply called the S&P) is based on the value of five hundred companies. Because this is a much larger cross section of the stock market (it includes many mid-sized firms as well as the industrial giants), the S&P is a good indicator of the direction of the market and the U.S. economy. However, the Dow is still the most commonly followed index, and the current Dow level is the number most people have in mind when they ask, "How did the market do today?"

How Stock Prices Rise

Most women—and most men—aren't used to buying things that grow in value. Your car, your clothes, your appliances all decline in value from the minute you buy them until, eventually, they're worth nothing and have to be thrown away. Investing in stocks is a different matter and requires a very different psychology.

Let me tell you a story that will illustrate how the stock market works.

About two years ago, my husband and I flew to Aspen for a ski vacation. He was flipping through a flight magazine when he suddenly stopped and blurted out, "Joanie, look. These are your earrings!" I leaned over, looked at the picture, and read the description, and sure enough, they were my earrings—a beautiful and distinctive set of Mobe pearls with a gold shield and a few small diamonds. I read further and saw that they had been designed by the same artist as mine.

Both Ron and I were amazed to see the earrings because I had purchased the lovely pair a decade earlier from my favorite jeweler, Sacks, in Philadelphia for $260. Now here they were for sale at a jewelry story in Aspen—the ski resort where we were headed.

Naturally, we were curious. When we landed in Aspen, we visited the jewelry store selling them and found out the new price, $2,200—for the same earrings by the same artist!

What happened to my jewelry is what happened to stock when the Dow rose from 800 to over 8,000: The price rose when more people wanted to buy it. The market rewards the patient investor who buys something of value and holds it until more people recognize its worth.

Furthermore, the stock market is a more powerful and reliable source of value growth than the jewelry market for several reasons. The value of a share of stock is based on the value of the company it represents. If the company is well run, its sales and profits will grow, and the value of its shares will rise. The continued growth of the U.S. and world economies is an engine that helps drive companies.

Think about it: If you own shares of Disney, every baby born represents a potential new consumer of Disney products—movies, toys, videos, vacations. And each new customer has a positive impact on Disney's bottom line—and on the value of your stock.

We have a saying at Take Charge Financial!—"Put your canoe in the river and float." That means, invest your money and you'll move along just fine with the currents of the stock market. Certainly, the market has ups and downs, but the downs are minuscule compared to its historic pattern of growth. The Dow has climbed steadily and relentlessly—it's the economic event of our lifetime. It's never approached zero, as a few doomsayers would have us believe. It hiccups once in a while. That's when many people run scared, tip their canoes, and swim to shore. Just remember the most significant characteristic of the stock market: Its history is a remarkable, insatiable, proven climb. You don't have to outsmart it—you just need to go with it. You have to get into the stream, though, to feel the momentum of the currents.

But what about those market "dips," when the Dow drops 50 or 100 points in a day and the price of your favorite stock is off by as much as a few dollars a share? What do you do when this happens? Don't run scared. Instead, love those dips!

Think of it this way. If you walk into a department store and see a dress you've wanted on sale, you don't look at it and say, "Yech! That's junk now because they've reduced the price. I wouldn't think of buying it!" No. A huge smile would probably wrap around your face as you reach for your wallet and think, "Wow! How great. What a terrific value. My favorite dress is half price. I probably should get two!" Well, the same is true of the stock market. If you believed a stock or mutual fund was a value before its price dropped, it's still a value; only now, it's a better one. In fact, when the market drops, I call it a "half-year liquidation sale." After you buy these "sale" stocks, keep them until they become popular again. Sometime later, you might sell them and realize a nice profit from your shopping spree.

Do you recall October 19, 1987? It was the day the media blurted out that the stock market "crashed." The Dow plunged more than 508 points as nervous investors sold their stocks. Well, I don't believe in "crashes." These market adjustments are wonderful "liquidation sales," and history proves that when you buy during a time when others are *fearful,* and hold on until investors are no longer panicky, you will eventually harvest rewards. If you purchased stocks at the great sale of October 19, 1987, you're extremely happy because the Dow has more than recovered and has gained enormous strength since then. Following this day, the Dow steadily climbed, setting a new record on January 2, 1990, when it closed at 2,810.15. A year later, the Dow closed at over 3,000. By 1996, it reached a high of over 6,000 and by 1997, it climbed to 8,000. So the next time you hear "crash," just smile and say, "Great. I'm going shopping!"

Words like "crash"—words that grab headlines—can swing you into that "fear and greed" mentality of Wall Street. Remember, selling when the market declines only fattens the broker's commission check. That's not sensible investing. When the market is down, the wealth-building strategy is to buy more or do nothing. Historically, the market has always bounced back from its falls to even higher heights.

The average annual growth of the stock market since the very beginning of the U.S. market, including all of its dips, is about 12 percent. In a given year, returns can run as high as 35 percent, as did the returns from many mutual funds in 1995. You won't expect every year to produce a return as high as those in 1995, but statistically, there is a one-out-of-two chance that you will receive better than a 15 percent return in the market in any given year.

Few things in life are as reliable as the growth of the stock market. That's why stocks are such an essential part of your Money Machine.

Moving into the Market

Now, taking that first step is a challenge for many of us, because we've been led to believe that investing involves risk. Yes, you can lose money in the market. But with the right approach, there'll be smooth sailing, as long as you don't gamble away your money as Wall Street would have you do. By now you see that the real risk is doing nothing, because then you'll have zip for your future.

If you have any negative feelings about the market, and many women do, it's probably because of a handful of bad-boy—and bad-girl—brokers, who give the industry a black eye. It's not the stock market—it's those roguish, rascally retailers. The problem is not the message, but the messenger. I talk to many women who say they don't trust the brokerage community because they see investing as a win/lose process: Someone else wins; they lose.

When I worked as an investment banker, municipal bond trader, and broker, I saw how consumers were treated in what was, and largely continues to be, a white-male-dominated, ego-driven business. Let me tell you, my pet frog got more respect than most investors got from their brokers. In Chapter 10, I'll talk about how to find a financial advocate who will encourage and support the growth of your Money Machine.

But it's essential to understand and stay focused on the importance of the stock market to your financial growth and your Money Machine. There is no magic in the consistent results the stock market has provided, and its benefits reward *everyone*—when it hands out its returns to investors, it does not discriminate by gender, race, or religion. Over the years, the market has created tremendous wealth for many people, despite some corrections or dips. And what's exciting about the market is that every time it dips, you can count on it coming back even stronger and reaching higher levels.

Knowing When a Stock Is Valuable

How do you know when you're buying a stock of value? Do you simply trot after the herd as it races toward the hottest technology company because someone told you that you could "make a killing"? Do you put on a blindfold and play a game of "pin the tail on the stock"? How do you know if a company is going to grow well?

The first thing to remember is that when you invest in stocks, what you're doing is investing in a company; you become a shareholder. That means that when you buy IBM stock, you actually own a part of the company. And when you own a mutual fund, you own many pieces of different companies. Therefore, when deciding what stocks to buy, think about what companies you'd like to own.

To begin with, use your intuition and womanly insight. Ask yourself, what do people need in order to be happy, productive, and comfortable? What do many people in the world yearn to own? Do they yearn for items that you and I take for granted? What do you see that other people value, not just for the moment but for the long term? The companies that create this value are those that are likely to grow and profit.

Invest in companies you know about: Check out the clothes you wear, the car you drive, the electronic equipment you use, the restaurants you frequent. When you go to see a movie, which movie studio has consistent box-office hits? When you travel to another country or another part of the United States, look around and see what's happening and which companies are providing what's most badly needed or wanted, whether it's telephones, computers, pharmaceuticals, or blue jeans.

RIDING THE INVESTMENT WAVES

When you put your canoe into the investment waters, it's really splendid when a wave or swell comes along to push you forward. You might even get a rush as you cascade over the waters. I like to call this the "wave theory." The idea is to get in front of an investment wave and then ride it all the way to profitability. You won't have to paddle a whole lot with this type of momentum.

It's easy to see the great investment waves of the past. If we look back to the early 1970s, hindsight shows us that a great wave to catch was the burgeoning computer, semiconductor, and software industries. Consumers wanted to spend their money to join the computer revolution. I spent a lot of money on computers during that decade—more than I did on cars. That says something, particularly since computers, which people flocked to purchase, were brand new. The question to ask now is, what are the "waves" of the future, and which ones should you get in front of?

Here are some waves I see:

Between 1990 and 2010, the number of Americans over sixty-five will double. This group uses health care the most, and they will create an enormous demand for companies to produce goods and services to meet the critical health-care needs of our society. Health care is a high priority and a long-term trend. The price of health-care stocks took a tumble in 1995 as the nation debated nationalized health care and how to change our national delivery system, and as HMOs, with their new approach to cost cutting, spread. As a result, there was a liquidation sale in health-care stocks, but the long-term prospects for the industry remain great. Innovative people are going to figure out how to profitably provide health services to a hugely growing segment of the population. Thus, the value of worldwide health-care companies is sure to grow.

A second wave is the spread of telecommunications. If you've been to Europe, you may have noticed there are few Touch-Tone phones. The business of providing updated equipment to European telephone users is a likely growth industry. And in Mexico, until August 1996, Teléfonos de México S.A. (TeleMex) had a lock on all long-distance calls. Its forty-eight-year-old monopoly ended when competing Avantel S.A., with an investment of about $900 million, started its network, which links thirty-three of Mexico's largest cities. Because of this increased competition, you can expect telecommunications in Mexico to grow even more. In the United States, almost 58 out of 100 people have a phone; in Mexico, only 8 out of 100; in Brazil, only 7 out of 100; and in China, only 1.5 out of 100. All of that is changing—and we haven't even talked about how computers and satellite technology will expand telecommunications even further.

Does it matter that Mexico devalued its peso in December 1995 and pushed down the stock price of TeleMex? No. That's because telecommunications has proven to be too much of an opportunity. Even now, TeleMex holds on to most of the market. And how long do you think it will take to satisfy all the telecommunications demands of the world and then go back and upgrade them? Is it worth it? This should give you a clue: In 1995, China spent $8 billion on telephone lines and infrastructure. So you could pick a mutual fund specializing in telecommunications stocks as an excellent wave to ride.

Here's another wave to think about: As the Berlin Wall fell and the Soviet Union disintegrated, new markets opened. What will be the growth industries of the future for Germans and Russians? First, they want essential services, like health care, telephones, and materials to build homes and businesses. They also want consumer products, especially items that Americans love and use—blue jeans, beer, Coca-Cola, electronics, Nike sneakers. Western companies—including computer businesses—are aggressively pursuing these opportunities in the former communist bloc. Invest in the stock of these companies.

Other waves of the future are natural resources and waste management. Companies have already begun explorations in Russia to tap into newly found natural resources. This could also be a folder in the stock drawer of your investment file cabinet.

Not all investment waves are obvious. You'll always use your feelings, intuitions, and any insights and observations you soak up on your way through life to pick the right industries. But also read, think, and, if you're so inclined, do research. Pick up your local newspaper or scan a national paper, such as *The New York Times, The Wall Street Journal, Investor's Business Daily,* or *Barron's,* to see what's happening elsewhere in the world.

Read magazines—not only newsmagazines, but also, for example, entertainment magazines. When three titans of film and entertainment—Jeffrey Katzenberg (Disney), filmmaker Steven Spielberg, and David Geffen (MCA)—join to form their own company, bells might go off in your head. All three men were already megasuccesses before they united to form DreamWorks SKG. Maybe their stock is worth looking into when it's made public.

Or how about the new Internet software, like Java and Netscape, that you keep reading about? Or pay attention to those fashion magazines—who's on the rise, just as Chanel was more than a half century ago with classic clothes and designs with universal appeal, clothes and designs that are likely to be with us for decades? Even Ralph Lauren is now a publicly traded stock. Gossip columns and people-in-the-news pages often provide grist for investment mills: Read about who's having dinner with whom to discuss new products or mergers.

Finally, don't be afraid to tackle the business pages of newspapers or national newsmagazines. Often, they have lively reports on companies that are worth investigating.

PICKING A STOCK

Beyond the ideas that intuition and research give you, you must develop objective criteria for selecting a particular company and buying its stock to build your wealth. I'm going to tell you about the model my firm uses to evaluate stocks. I'll run through the criteria so that you can ask the same types of questions a fund manager asks before buying a stock for her or his fund. This will also give you a good idea of the type of evaluation you need to make if you decide to fill your Money Machine with individual stocks. I think after reading this, you'll be inclined to choose mutual funds for most of the investments for your Money Machine. But if choosing stocks intrigues you, this will show you how it's done.

The basic rule of thumb:

> You want a quality company whose stock is priced within an acceptable range for you, one whose stock price can grow to give you an annual return of about 15 percent so that its price doubles in five years.

Why five years at about 15 percent or better? Because you want an investment that grows the volume of your Money Machine and, as the Rule of 72 shows, you'll double your investment in five years (72 divided by 14.7 is 5). It's a slightly ambitious but very achievable goal for the smart stock market investor.

The stock evaluation model is basically a "filtering" system that asks the following questions about a company and its stock:

- Is it a **quality company**?
- What is the **right price** to buy this stock at?
- What is your **subjective evaluation** of the company?

Let's examine these questions.

First: *Is it a **quality company?*** The most important consideration is whether the company you have in mind makes a profit and whether it offers goods and services that you believe will make it more profitable in the future. It's also important to know whether the company is well managed. Finally, it is important to know whether its leaders can anticipate future trends in its industry. How can you determine this? Read whatever you can, and ask questions. Go to your local library and peruse *The Wall Street Journal, Fortune, Business Week,* or *The New York Times,* or log onto the Internet and look up the company. See what is written about its managers and how they handle the company's helm. You can also read a copy of a company's annual report, which you can obtain from any brokerage house or the company itself.

At my firm, we take the "quality filter" several steps further to evaluate stock purchases. We also look at reports issued by Value Line: a company's sales and earnings history and its industry ranking—how it compares to other companies in the same industry; its projected earnings; timeliness—how fast, according to stock analysts, the price of the stock will increase in the next year; safety—how much, according to analysts, the price is expected to fluctuate in the next year; the company's long-term debt (too much is not good); and growth trends in the industry.

Value Line is a research company that issues reports based upon data secured from a company and assesses what that company's earnings and profits should be in the future. Value Line is a marvelous resource for any investor, and its company reports are available in almost every public library. If you're considering buying stock in a company, check out the most recent *Value Line Report* on that company—you'll surely learn all types of worthwhile information.

Also check out various Internet sites for information, such as www.stocksmart.com or www.techstocks.com. You'll have to decide for yourself how deeply you want to analyze a company's performance. Some people find it a fascinating endeavor. If you are such a person, there are books, magazines, and other resources that can show you how to evaluate company stocks in which you are interested. If this is not your cup of tea, you can go the mutual fund route.

Once we determine that a company's stock is a good investment, we move on to the next filter.

Second: *What is the **right price** to buy this stock at?* Here our goal is to determine at what price we will buy the stock, at what price we will continue to hold the stock, and at what price we will sell it. It's very important to know your strategy before you buy a stock. We use a mathematical formula based on information from Value Line to estimate how much the stock price is likely to increase. This helps us not only to decide whether we should buy the stock, but also to reevaluate our investment and to establish when we should take our profits and sell the stock.

How do you decide when your stock no longer has the potential to grow in price and it's time to consider selling it? You'll ride its wave as long as you think there are growth opportunities. If you think the wave is diminishing, then get off and catch the next one. Let's say a decade or so ago, you purchased stock in a company that made high-quality Betamax videocassettes. The video market was beginning to boom, and you were right there to catch the wave. But Beta went nowhere and was quickly replaced by VHS. So you might have sold Beta stock and caught the VHS wave. A few years ago, you noticed that laser discs were being made of your favorite movies. You noticed also that they cost a lot less than videocassettes and produced superior copies of films. Now DVDs (digital video-discs) have the potential to take over the video market. Your video-cassette stock did well, but now you want to catch the laser disc or DVD wave. This may be the time to sell one stock and to buy another.

Furthermore, your videocassette stock may have hit a plateau—a price that it's unlikely to exceed. Just as you purchased the stock at a low price before everyone else was buying it, you might want to sell it now that everyone else *is* buying. You'll be able to ascertain this by simply checking the stock listings and monitoring the rate of change for a few weeks. You can even log onto the Internet at www.NASDAQ.com or www.DBC.com for stock quotes.

As you see, when you examine the stock price, considerations about buying and selling are important.

In order to evaluate the price of a stock, my firm also considers the following:

(a) Whether a company pays out less than 50 percent of its earnings in dividends. You're looking for a company that puts most of its earnings back into the company to finance future growth rather than chisels away its profits by doling out hefty dividends to shareholders. You stand to earn more on your investment if the company can increase its value because it was wise enough to reinvest its profits in the company.

(b) Sales-earnings comparisons, also provided by Value Line. You want to invest in a company whose profits are growing at the same rate as sales, or better.

(c) Estimated high and low prices—that is, the probable high and low of a stock's price over the next five years. Value Line provides such estimates. You can also get a research report with similar estimates from a stock analyst; ask your broker to send you his or her research department's report on the company in which you're interested, or check the Internet.

Naturally, these are just estimates; investment analysts, like weather forecasters, are often wrong. Still, the weather report can be helpful before going out in the morning.

Third: *What is your **subjective evaluation** of the company?* This is when your gut gets to speak. How do you *feel* about a company, based on everything you've learned? And just as important, do you *believe* in the company's products and its mission? For example, I wouldn't buy stock in a firearms company or a tobacco firm, regardless of profits, because I don't like the nature of their businesses. This is a visceral objection, not a fiscal consideration. It's part of the economic power I talked about earlier: You get to vote both as a consumer and as an investor. But if you like and respect a company's product and how the company governs itself, go for it.

Your subjective evaluation can also include an assessment of information from other sources, like annual reports, newspaper and magazine articles, and so on. If you see any red flags, such as major lawsuits, internal bickering, unrest, or anything else that might derail a company from its positive mission, then you might ask yourself whether the company's stock is a worthwhile investment. For example, Columbia-HCA Healthcare Corp.'s stock took a deep plunge following federal allegations of Medicare fraud. If you know someone who works for the company, ask about morale. How optimistic is the atmosphere at the firm? Are the best people staying or leaving? Answers to questions like these can tell a lot about a company's long-term prospects.

These three evaluation filters are essential to buying stock and will also help you to broaden your knowledge of its industry. This is the fundamental groundwork that it takes to buy the right stock—not a hot tip. If you're still serious about buying individual stocks, check out other resource materials that go into more depth and continue to increase your knowledge about buying and selling stocks. And/or you can take a different direction: You can choose a mutual fund and leave the stock selection up to the fund manager. If you belong to an investment club, you can get a similar model for stock selection from the National Association of Investors Corporation.

CHOOSING A MUTUAL FUND

There's a universe of mutual funds on the market—in fact, more funds than individual stocks are listed on the New York Stock Exchange, American Stock Exchange, and Pacific Stock Exchange. But many of the more than eight thousand mutual funds available to you *don't* perform as well as the overall market.

You can go to several places to check out good funds. Your broker or adviser can tell you about several selections that fit your criteria. You can also check out the financial pages in your newspaper for mutual fund listings, or you can surf the 'net to come up with some options. The most comprehensive list, though, can be found at your public library in the Morningstar report. Much like Value Line reports for stocks, Morningstar is a reference for all mutual funds. It includes information about each fund's portfolio, its manager, its historical performance, and other helpful data. Morningstar rates mutual funds on a scale of one to five stars. The number of stars given to a particular fund does not relate to how well it will perform for the investor in the future, however.

One way to sort through the galaxy of funds is to pick a good fund family, then decide on two or three investment waves you'd like to ride and find a fund that has performed as well as the stock market.

Ask yourself what you see as the waves of the future. If you were to make a list, would you include health care? Telecommunications? Financial services? Would your list include small and growing companies and international corporations?

Let's say you've put together a list representing the investment waves of the future and you've decided to seek funds that concentrate on investing in health care, telecommunications, and financial services, and that also invest internationally. How will you know what types of stocks are in a specific fund? Sometimes the fund name will give you a clue. You may also request a copy of the fund prospectus, which will give you information about the fund, including where it invests its money. After a little sleuthing, you'll be able to determine whether the fund supports your waves of the future.

If the fund does reflect your investment philosophy, you'll need information on how well the fund has grown over the past five years. You can obtain a fund history from the fund manager, your broker, or Morningstar. You can also log on to the Internet at www.Galt.com for mutual fund prices and historical performance information. Find out the fund's year-to-date return, as well as its one-year return, three-year return, and five-year return. Keep in mind the Rule of 72 to determine how fast your money should double in the fund. The fund's history gives you an idea of how the fund has been managed in the past. If you're looking at three health-care funds, and if one of them has a consistently better return than the other two, then you'll know that the first fund has done a better job choosing health-care stocks.

You can also review the fund family. One fund family might offer anywhere from three to over one hundred different mutual funds. So it's possible to find health-care, telecommunications, and financial services funds all within the same family. Unless you have a substantial sum of money to invest, you're better off investing in only one family, because if you choose to move your money from one mutual fund within that family to another in the same family, there will generally be no charge. So if you invest in the American small cap fund and then decide that the place to be is in the Europe small cap fund, you can easily make the move.

When you buy a mutual fund, another consideration is the type of sales charge, or "load," you will be asked to pay. Many funds use letters of the alphabet to designate different types of loads. If you buy *A* shares, a sales charge is deducted up front from the money you invest. Thus, if you invest $1,000, the actual amount that goes into the fund may be only $970—$1,000 minus a 3 percent sales charge.

If you buy *B* shares, all of the money you invest goes into the fund. However, a load is assessed when you sell your shares, unless you remain in the fund family for a specified period, usually five or more years.

If you buy *C* shares, a load (usually 1 percent of the value of your holdings) is assessed each year you're invested in the fund.

No-load funds are not necessarily cheaper than load funds, because of annual fees and charges that are included in no-loads.

International Perspective

I have purposely discussed the stock market in international terms. It is no longer sensible for an investor to restrict herself to the U.S. stock market. Think globally—the U.S. market is not necessarily the best and certainly not the only one.

Did you know that from 1985 to 1995, the U.S. stock market ranked among the five best-performing stock markets in the world for only three years? In 1995, our stock market's performance ranked second, and from 1991 through 1992, it ranked third. In the seven other years, it didn't even make the cut. But stock markets in Spain, Switzerland, Japan, Germany, Austria, Norway, and Hong Kong did. Rapidly growing economies in Asia and Europe fueled those markets, and the Third World and the former Iron Curtain countries are showing signs of becoming similarly dynamic. So you can easily see that investing internationally is a key strategy for growing your money.

The best way to invest internationally, though, is through mutual funds that offer international portfolios. For example, you can buy telecommunications mutual funds that invest worldwide. The basket of stocks in such a fund could include Pacific Bell, AT&T, the phone company of Brazil, and the phone company of Australia.

Learning to Love the Market

And by pursuing your investments domestically or internationally, the most important consideration is to use the stock market to build your Money Machine. It is the best proven wealth builder, and it will ably take care of your financial needs.

Think of this. Think of the stock market as you would a lover. You must build a relationship that will survive the ups and downs of investing. The same patience and steadfastness that are essential to a relationship are also essential to investing in the market. If you headed for the door every time your partner yelled at you, you'd constantly be starting over. Maybe you'd have blown what could have been a very good relationship. And if you had never tried again, you'd have missed out on a potentially wonderful part of life.

Just as you have to ride out some hard times with a partner or husband in order to build a committed, long-term bond, so, too, do you have to weather the blustery times of investing—to commit seriously to your investment strategy in order to experience long-term success. It is the woman who is willing to watch, wait, and work on the challenges and difficult areas, and to assess where the relationship is going, who eventually begins to experience the real potential of the union. Similarly, it is the patient investor, not the speculator, hunch player, or panicked seller, who reaps the most benefits from the upward trends of the stock market.

8

More Investment Choices: Bonds and Real Estate

The Bond Drawer
The Real Estate Drawer

THE BOND DRAWER

Bonds are not useful for growing your Money Machine. So why does your file cabinet have a bond drawer? For two reasons. First, because in the allocation of your cash, you may choose to safely tuck some money in Treasuries—U.S. government-assured, fixed-rate-of-return securities. This is a means of guaranteeing the return of your money on a certain date and for a known interest rate. You may choose to secure 20 percent of your portfolio this way if you're conservative. And second, because bonds may become important later in your life, when you reach a stage where you want to receive a fixed amount of income that's regularly paid to you.

But the bond market is not the place to be if you want to repeatedly double your money so that you can reach your Money Machine goal. Under most economic circumstances, bond rates hardly keep you ahead of inflation. The interest they pay is too low, and it takes too long for your money to grow. However, you can safely stash some money in Treasuries and you'll want to know enough about bonds so that you can decide wisely should a broker or adviser ever encourage you to include them in your portfolio.

What is a bond? For our purposes, a bond is any security that pays you interest for a specified period and then repays you the face value of the security. When you buy stock, you become a part owner of the company. When you buy a bond, you become a lender; the company, bank, or government agency issuing the bond is borrowing money from you for a certain length of time and agreeing to pay you a certain amount of interest for it.

Examples of bonds include certificates of deposit (CDs), government savings bonds, corporate bonds, municipal bonds, and Treasury notes. The difference between them is their time span and their interest rates—some pay higher interest than others.

For example, let's take a look at CDs, which are jokingly called "certificates of depreciation" these days. When you take the (usually very low) interest rate and subtract inflation, the real rate of return is sometimes *negative*. In other words, the value of your investment is shrinking over time rather than growing. And remember the Rule of 72, which governs the process of doubling your money: 72 divided by negative-something does not work very well! In 1975, which boasted the highest average annual CD rate—15.79 percent—after subtracting inflation and taxes, the real rate of return was –2.43 percent.

So be wary of bonds as an investment, especially during the years when you're working to grow your Money Machine. They won't serve you well.

Bond History

For much of the twentieth century, investors looked to municipal bonds to provide income for their futures. These bonds are issued by states, cities, counties, and other local governments as a way to borrow money in order to build projects and to provide for other government needs. Because they are government issued, municipals had some special advantages. Bonds provided tax-free income, and if they were issued as bearer bonds—bonds that are not shown on the investor's tax return—they could easily be given to someone else without incurring any tax liability. For years, when inflation rates were low, these bonds worked very nicely because they yielded a semiannual income you could count on to pay daily expenses. For many investors, municipal bonds provided a predictable stream of tax-free income.

In the mid-1970s, municipal bond interest rates reached all-time highs; then, in the early 1990s, they reached historical lows. People found that the prices of their bonds varied widely. Also, as part of the tax reform of the early 1980s, all bonds were required to be issued as registered bonds: The bond trustee must record the investor's name and address, and municipal bond income is reportable on tax returns. (Even when the muni interest itself continued to be tax free, investors were indirectly hurt because their overall income increased and, thus, pushed them into a higher tax bracket.) So municipal bonds lost some of the features that had previously made them such an attractive investment.

I cut my teeth in the investment banking world by structuring bond transactions for municipal projects. I was responsible for packaging multimillion-dollar bond programs; the bonds were then sold to individual investors.

Soon after I entered the bond market in 1975, I saw municipal bond interest rates reach more than 15 percent, and they were tax free. Today, they are down to the 4–5 percent range, which is the low end of where they've been historically. One key to understanding bonds is that when interest rates rise, the price of an existing bond falls. How does this work? Well, suppose you have a bond that pays 5 percent interest, and you want to sell it to me, but the prevailing interest rate is 7 percent. Therefore, I am going to buy your 5 percent bond only if you sell it to me below your cost to compensate for the bond's lower interest rate. Today, interest rates have more room to rise than to fall, and every rise in interest rates means a loss in value for bonds. This means you're likely to lose money in a bond investment in today's interest-rate environment.

Have you noticed that mortgage interest rates are historically low? This gives you a clue. They mirror the bond market. If rates were historically high but were heading downward, your bond's price would rise. It was certainly not such a bad idea to buy municipal bonds when their interest rates were 15 percent, which was a historical high. Chances were that interest rates would fall and the price of your bond would rise. Today, the opposite situation exists.

When I created my own municipal bond company, I traded large blocks of bonds. We helped the city of Chicago, for example, to create bonds that provided money to build new schools and airport and sports facilities. We owned those bonds; we then sold them to bond funds. We owned about $8 million in California state bonds when, in 1994, the chairman of the Federal Reserve Bank unexpectedly hiked the Fed Funds interest rate. I hate to tell you what happened to the price of our bonds. Trust me, it wasn't a pretty picture. It was a challenging situation, but we got through it and went on to more fruitful opportunities.

To help me with situations like these, I sought the counsel of a wise and wonderful older man named Wayne, who had spent fortyseven years in the municipal bond business. He had retired from Merrill Lynch, and during his career, he had once been in charge of its West Coast bond trading department. Wayne was one of those special men who encouraged me to be more than I thought I could be, and who sometimes really leveled with me when I most needed to hear the truth.

We were sitting in my office one day chatting about the bond business, and our conclusion made us laugh: We surmised that we couldn't understand why people would want to own bonds! Even if you get a good tax-free rate of 10 percent for a municipal bond, when interest rates go down, the municipality may buy back your bond, so that it can refinance its debt at a lower rate. (This is known as "calling in" a bond.) And if you buy a bond with a 5 percent rate and interest rates go up, you're stuck with a low rate and a bond whose value is sorely diminished.

Are Bonds Safe?

Some people, however, still believe that bonds are safer and more secure than stocks. Sadie, the writer I'd met at the Ranch, called me one day, somewhat troubled about one of her investments. She had successfully grown about $35,000 in mutual funds. But her broker had suddenly advised her to dump two of her mutual funds and to get into the bond market. The brokerage firm seemed to think it was the right time to make such a move. This didn't feel comfortable to Sadie. Both of her mutual funds had outperformed the stock market, but her broker persuaded her to drop them and switch her investments to a bond fund that dramatically underperformed the stock market.

Along the way, her broker had not provided Sadie with any knowledge about bonds or how they work; she was not educated about her choices. Hooked by his advice, she took a dive. Sadie sadly watched the price of her bonds plummet. Once again, a woman was following her White Knight instead of controlling her own financial future. At least this time, she paid attention to that uncomfortable feeling in the pit of her stomach and questioned the advice she'd been receiving. Sadie asked me to examine her portfolio and to help her sort through her various investments. We'll get back to Sadie and her bond dilemma later.

There are periods when it is better to own bonds than stocks—usually relatively short intervals when the performance of the stock market and trends in interest rates are such that bonds outperform stocks. Unfortunately, it's virtually impossible to recognize such intervals in advance.

Some people claim they can "time" the markets—or move their investments from cash to stocks to bonds according to changes in market activity so as to get the best possible results. But when I worked on Wall Street, I found that, many times, the forecasts of the "experts" were exactly the opposite of what actually happened. If the weatherman on the six o'clock news incorrectly predicts a sunny day and you go out without an umbrella, the worst thing that happens is a horrible hair day. But if you base an investment move on someone's erroneous forecast of interest-rate changes or economic upheaval, you can lose big time. If you are out of the stock market for only a few days in some years, you can miss major gains for the year.

No one knows what the stock market is going to do. If they did, they would all go home because they would have collected their riches. The truth is, most people in the securities business don't have a clue. But making predictions about market timing is a fine way to move customers' money and is frequently a means to generate commissions. The brokers may benefit, but you don't.

This is what happened to Sadie. Her bonds declined in value while the stock market rose to glorious new heights, all because a particular brokerage firm had a theory about "market trends." Or maybe it was just a particular broker who had the theory. No matter. Sadie is the one who had to live with the results.

The sound wealth-building strategy is to stay with the proven and historically predictable long-term returns of the stock market and not be persuaded to move hither and yon.

Bonds are useful only when you want to establish a fixed amount of interest that is paid to you annually so you can secure your investment. Even then, they are a "safe" investment only when you buy an individual bond (for example, a bond from an issue for your local school district or a Treasury note) and hold it until its stated maturity, for example, through ten years to repayment. This way, you will get back all of your money. Even if the bond is "called in," you'll still be repaid the full amount of your investment. This is how bonds earned a reputation for safety.

Trading into and out of bonds, or using bond funds, is a different approach, and not a secure one. When you take this approach, you are subject to market risk, and changes in interest rates will affect the daily value of your bond. You are not assured that you will get all your money back.

I will say this again: Do not use the bond drawer to build your Money Machine. By browsing through what the stock drawer has to offer, you'll make your financial life a lot easier.

Now let's talk about the real estate drawer.

THE REAL ESTATE DRAWER

The seventies and eighties were the golden age of real estate. Savvy New Yorkers and other city dwellers scooped up for a mere $60,000 three-bedroom apartments that today are worth as much as $1 million. In California, first-time homeowners who lucked out with that cute little cottage for $75,000 sold it within a year or two for two or three times as much. Not a bad turn of the money. The catch phrase was "flip it," meaning "buy it and sell it fast."

For a while, it worked: The market climbed to unimaginable heights. Then the nineties came with a very big reality jolt. The same desirable co-ops and condos that were almost "flipped" into infinity became immovable objects of regret. You couldn't give those properties away; many owners sold at enormous losses, if they sold at all.

People were treating their houses, condos, and co-ops as if they were a buy-at-one-price-and-sell-at-a-higher-price part of their Money Machine. But remember, your home is not part of your real estate drawer. It doesn't generate cash, and therefore it cannot be a source of the money you'll eventually need to live on after you stop working. At best, your home will eventually be paid off and won't be part of your monthly expenses.

So just what is in the real estate drawer? Income-producing property, like apartment dwellings, stores, office space, houses for rent, and so forth. Is real estate a worthwhile investment for you? It depends on *you*. Being a landlord requires more of your time than managing stock investments. And real estate is less liquid than stock and mutual fund investments. Real estate, unlike stocks and bonds, is sold in one-on-one transactions rather than in a vast, regulated open market; you may not immediately be able to sell a house or apartment should the need for cash arise.

Real estate prices are not expected to do as well in the next twenty years as they did in the 1970s and 1980s, although lately they have been on the upswing. The large number of immigrants who entered the United States in the 1990s is partly responsible for the boost in the real estate market; so are the last of the baby boomers, who decided to buy property late in life. Still, the gargantuan sales of a decade or two ago are unlikely. You just might turn a profit if you sell real estate in midwestern states, like Ohio, Michigan, and Indiana, but you may not be so lucky in other areas, like the East and West Coasts.

Nonetheless, real estate has its advantages as an investment. That beach cottage in Ocean City, Maryland, or the country cabin near Asheville, North Carolina, or the ranch in Wyoming, where you plan to summer, or the ski retreat in Deer Valley, Utah, are attractive and desirable properties in their own right. If you consider renting them out for all or part of the year, then you'll generate income and your Money Machine will appreciate, even as you enjoy a few weeks each year in the house yourself. If you can charge more in rent than you pay out each month for your mortgage and overhead costs, you'll have a healthy flow of cash that will keep your Money Machine purring.

A good source of real estate income can be commercial properties, such as apartment dwellings, stores, office space, and so forth. But "location, location, location" is still the key. If an area or neighborhood has a glut of rentals, you could get stuck. Months could go by without renters, and this makes investing in rental properties more risky than investing in a healthy mutual fund.

Two years ago, my husband, Ron, pointed out that we were spending a lot of money renting office space in two different locations for our two separate businesses. We discussed this and concluded that if we continued to pay rent to someone, that person would own a piece of real estate in fifteen years through our efforts. We asked ourselves, "Why not us?"

So we looked for a building that would suit our needs. We wanted to occupy 90 percent of the building so that a bad tenant wouldn't jeopardize our equity, and we wanted something unique, just to make the experience of owning and maintaining the building enjoyable. We wound up buying a wonderful hundred-year-old building listed in the National Register of Historic Places. Residents of our town affectionately call our building "The Castle." It was built by a brick mason for his sweetheart, who lived in Philadelphia. He hoped to marry her someday. Yes—she came, they married, and they moved into The Castle. My office is in what was once the living room. I imagine that female spirits in their bustled dresses are looking over my shoulder and marveling at how far women have come in taking charge of their financial futures!

We will pay for the building over time. Then later, when we no longer need it for our businesses, we'll rent it out, and the rent will be part of the income generated from our Money Machine.

If you are a small-business owner in a similar situation, financing is available from the Small Business Administration that makes buying this kind of building easier. If you have a business with a proven track record, and if you plan to purchase real estate, check out the SBA.

Another piece of real estate that fits nicely into a Money Machine is the three-bedroom house owned by friends of mine who live near the beach in Santa Cruz, California. They rent it out during the school year to students from the University of Santa Cruz in order to pay the mortgage, and they get to enjoy it themselves during the summer. Once their mortgage is fully paid up, rental income and the value of the house will be part of their Money Machine.

A man we know named Mike has purchased ten houses in various parts of California over the past fifteen years. He rents them out to families; he even rents out part of the house in which he lives. He's definitely devised a long-term plan for building wealth by sorting through the opportunities in the real estate drawer. He decided also that it was worth it to pay others to oversee his properties so that he wouldn't have to travel in the middle of the night to fix the water heater.

Other friends have a successful income-producing property in Philadelphia. They purchased a building, moved into the top floor, and opened an art gallery on the bottom floor.

Some might say, "You need capital to buy a building. How would I get it?" If you have an established business, plan to occupy the building, and can demonstrate that you will generate enough cash to meet monthly debt service on a mortgage, investors will be willing to make mortgage loans. Run an ad in your local newspaper—you might be surprised at the responses you'll receive. But you'll have to be prepared to do the legwork, like identifying the property and its costs and presenting your payment plan for the building. Look at it this way: You'll become your own investment banker, and you will pocket cash that would otherwise be someone else's fee.

If you do decide to buy real estate for investment purposes, you will also want to pay off the principal on your mortgage as quickly as possible. This will dramatically cut your mortgage payments, which go almost entirely to paying the bank its interest. You might think that it's okay to stretch out your payments because the interest is tax-deductible, but this makes the building cost you more, and this is money you could be investing instead of paying to the mortgage lender—cash you could be growing in your Money Machine. The investment income you could be generating is worth much more than the tax deduction.

Your Investment Options: The Bottom Line

You now have a clear picture of the investment options for your Money Machine: stocks, bonds, and real estate. The bottom line is that your Money Machine will most likely be centered largely on mutual funds. You might also build your wealth with some individual stocks and perhaps with one or two pieces of income-generating real estate. You'll do just fine, though, if you consistently steer your cash toward a variety of investment-wave mutual funds and/or stocks and monitor their performance. It's a safe, powerful way to grow your wealth, and one that is easy to get started in with an investment of as little as $500.

Now let's consider how you'll choose to be taxed, looking at the investment options in each of the three file cabinets.

9

Investment Strategies: Taxable, Tax-Deferred, and Tax-Free Choices

File Cabinet No. 1: Taxable Investments
File Cabinet No. 2: Qualified Plans
File Cabinet No. 3: The Private Pension Plan
Simplifying Your Investments

etty Scott arrived at my office cradling a large display of yellow tulips with thick green stems. They were a glorious deep yellow, like ripe lemons dangling from a tree on a sun-splashed day.

"I knew you'd appreciate these," she said with a wicked grin and an impish wink, referring to the harassment I had experienced in a Philadelphia investment office so long ago because of my desire to have yellow tulips on my desk.

"You know what," she said, alluding to that experience, "I'm here to change the trend, too. The trend I'm altering is my financial life. I'm going to create a new lifestyle for myself—financial ease."

Betty was aglow, as if some sort of positive electricity were rippling through her. I could tell instantly that she had made some changes for herself.

"So tell me what you've done," I said.

"I torched my Visa," she said with a huge laugh. "Women before me burned their bras. I burned my credit card. It felt good!"

"Good show. Now you're really taking charge." I gave Betty a hug and sat down with my yellow pad to jot down some notes. "Okay. Let's get to work. What do you have?"

"Well," she began, fingering some pages in a folder, "I have my 401(k) plan, which has about $25,000 in it, and an IRA I haven't funded for some time."

"How much do you have in the IRA?" I asked.

"I think about $5,000. I also have an insurance policy that my father gave me and $10,000 in my checking account. Would you please go over the file cabinets with me again and help me understand what my financial picture looks like? I need to see how these investments will fit into the drawers."

"No problem. Let's run through each of the file cabinets and see how it all sorts out for you," I said. "Our objective is to figure out how much cash will be coming to you in the future and what its source will be."

I pulled out my drawing of the three file cabinets and began to construct the landscape of Betty's financial life.

FILE CABINET NO. 1: TAXABLE INVESTMENTS

At the moment, Betty has no investments in this file cabinet. She does have some cash that is sitting uninvested in a "To Be Filed" basket next to the cabinet—the $10,000 in her checking account.

Let's say she did have investments in this file cabinet. What would they likely be? She might have a piece of rental property in her real estate drawer. She might also have opened a brokerage account and purchased some stock, which would be in her stock drawer. This type of investment account can be opened through a brokerage firm, an investment adviser, or even an on-line computer service that allows you access to purchasing stock.

Here's how opening a brokerage account works in our office. We give you three forms to fill out. The first asks for general information, like name, address, and Social Security number. The second form is an agreement of understanding that you're opening an account. The third is an IRS form that verifies your Social Security number for tax purposes. That's all there is to it.

Opening a brokerage account is as easy as opening a checking account at a bank, and once it's set up, you can deposit money into the account and use it to make purchases, like individual stocks and mutual funds. The account also includes a money market fund—an investment in short-term corporate debt that pays interest to shareholders. So as long as your cash remains in the account, it earns interest at the money market rate, which lately can range from about 3.5 to 6 percent per year.

Betty's cash is not earning interest in her checking account. By simply moving it into an investment account, money market interest will be generated. The highest money market rates are paid by brokerage firms, not banks. When you open your investment account, ask what the money market interest rate is. But remember, a money market fund is a short-term tool. Even though it's earning interest, I don't consider it an investment for your long-term financial growth. A money market account is simply a holding pen for your cash until you hatch an investment plan so your cash can build up your Money Machine.

That's where Betty is at the moment with the money she has in her checking account. Should she choose File Cabinet No. 1, 2, or 3 to invest this cash? We first discussed File Cabinet No. 1.

"How do you want to be taxed? Remember, this file cabinet is not protected from taxation. You are taxed across the board; dividends and interest are taxed, as is any gain from the sale of your investments," I said.

Betty frowned. "Frankly, I don't want to be taxed at all," she said.

"Of course not," I said with a laugh. "But before you get too concerned about giving up money to Uncle Sam, keep in mind that if you get a good return on your investment, you can afford to pay your taxes and still come out ahead. This file cabinet has its place, but we won't make any decisions right now. Let's see how it fits into your investment strategy and examine the other two file cabinets."

"Fair enough," Betty replied.

FILE CABINET NO. 2: QUALIFIED PLANS

Qualified plans are special accounts that Uncle Sam has agreed to defer taxing. These include traditional IRAs, 401(k) plans, 403(b) plans, company pension plans, Keoghs, and SEP-IRAs (simplified employee pensions). A SEP-IRA works like an IRA, but a SEP-IRA allows a self-employed person to make higher tax-deductible contributions. Self-employed people, as well as corporations and partnerships, may also use Keoghs. They permit employers to contribute up to 15 percent of all employees' compensation to an employee's saving plan. 401(k) plans, 403(b) plans, and company pension plans are also made available by employers.

If you use a qualified plan, your money goes into your plan tax free and grows tax free. However, you will pay a full tax at the regular income-tax rate when you withdraw money from any of these plans. If you've steadily mushroomed your account to, say, $250,000, that sum will be considered income when you withdraw it. Let's assume that your combined state and federal income tax rates will be roughly 40 percent. When you're ready to use that $250,000, you'll pay about $100,000 to Uncle Sam when you withdraw your money, and you'll realize only $150,000 of your investment.

Please remember the retirement income-tax myth we discussed in Chapter 3: "A sound investment program rests on the inevitability that the investor's taxes will be lower after stopping work." If you continue your current lifestyle, your tax rates are likely to be the same; they may be even higher, because tax rates are rising. If you are willing to significantly cut back on your spending and carve out a bare-bones existence, maybe you would have lower taxes.

We cannot predict what taxes will be when you reach the age at which you will plan to withdraw your contributions, but one thing is certain: Cash paid to you from your qualified plan will be treated as taxable income, as your salary was before you stopped working. Suppose you earned $50,000 a year when you were working and paid a certain tax on that income. If you have the same income later, you'll pay the same amount of tax on the $50,000 you withdraw from your traditional IRA once you stop working, assuming the tax rates are the same.

Qualified plans used to work better. That's because there was a time when people were more likely to be in a lower tax bracket during their nonworking years. The simplification of tax brackets and changes in the marginal tax rates (the highest tax rates that may be applied on income) have altered that reality. Furthermore, Congress controls the rules by which such plans work, and it has changed these rules hundreds of times in the past few years and thereby further complicated the picture. The bottom line is that between tax rates and the mercurial nature of the rules for qualified plans, it's difficult to know how much you'll receive from these plans when you're ready to withdraw your money and maintain your lifestyle.

Another challenge posed by qualified plans is that they often limit how much money can be contributed to them; thus they will often be unable to generate enough cash to maintain your preferred lifestyle. For example, if you're now forty-five years old and you can contribute only a maximum of $2,000 a year to an IRA, you won't have enough by the time you stop working. Even Keoghs and 401(k) plans, with their higher contribution limits, offer only a partial answer to designing your financial future.

Betty already has some qualified plan investments: She has $25,000 in her company 401(k) plan and $5,000 in her IRA. In which drawer of File Cabinet No. 2 does she have her 401(k) plan?

"Bonds," she said. "Government bonds. Someone once told me they were safe. But they seem so sluggish right now."

Betty was questioning the rate of return on her bond investment. She already suspected that bonds were not going to afford the best yield to grow her Money Machine. And her 401(k) is the largest bundle of cash she has working in her Money Machine. Her IRA, however, is in the stock drawer, invested in a mutual fund of world-wide stocks.

An investment or brokerage account for any of these qualified plans can be opened in a similar way to the process described for File Cabinet No. 1. In our office, we use the same three forms we use for investing in File Cabinet No. 1 plus a fourth form, which is an agreement of understanding that you're opening a qualified plan investment account. One of the government-imposed conditions of this type of account is that you can't withdraw money from your qualified plan until you reach age fifty-nine and a half. Your money will be taxed if you withdraw it before then, and the IRS will slap a 10 percent penalty on whatever funds are removed.

If you have an IRA at a bank, you can move the cash and investments in your IRA bank account to an IRA brokerage account. If you have left a company where you invested in a 401(k) plan or a pension plan, you can also transfer those investments to your IRA brokerage account. In both instances, you will have more flexibility in managing your money and more flexibility if you can consolidate two or more accounts into one. Don't worry about sacrificing diversification. Since you'll have a variety of investments, you won't have all your eggs in one basket. And you will receive information about your investments in a single monthly report rather than in two or more statements, which you would have to track down and interpret.

In the end, you'll probably want resources in each of the file cabinets to construct your Money Machine. This way you'll build a composite of investments with differing methods of taxation.

FILE CABINET NO. 3:
THE PRIVATE PENSION PLAN

Betty also has a beginning resource in this file cabinet: the cash value of the life insurance policy her father gave her.

"This file cabinet really has my attention," she said, "because it can give me back money tax free."

File Cabinet No. 3 can provide Betty's dignity money. This file cabinet allows you to grow money tax free and to withdraw it tax free—a real benefit in planning for the essentials of your future. Plus, unlike qualified plans, investments in this file cabinet impose no restrictions on who can own such an investment and no limits on how much you can invest.

This file cabinet is the private pension plan, which also is known by its more technical name, the flexible premium variable life insurance plan. From now on, we'll simply call it the "PPP." It is a combination of variable insurance and mutual funds. The primary aim of this investment is to take the best of what insurance has to offer— the ability to grow money tax free and to withdraw it tax free—and the best of what mutual funds have to offer—the historically high rate of return of stocks—and to unite them to grow money.

You might balk at the mere mention of insurance. But that response is based on an antiquated point of view. Many people believe that insurance should be bought only to provide a death benefit in order to protect those you love. This was the role of traditional insurance, and the power of insurance as an investment vehicle was indeed limited. However, insurance can now be used to bet that you will live a long time and will need some real *life* benefits. As you'll see, if you own mutual funds and insurance, you're missing an opportunity if they are not working together. If you do not combine them, you will pay the cost of insurance and the tax on the dividends and capital gains from your mutual fund. The wealth-building strategy is to unite the two and cut your costs.

The private pension plan file cabinet has the same three drawers as the other two cabinets: stocks, bonds, and real estate. You can own the same mutual fund in File Cabinet No. 1, and be taxed on both the dividends and profits you make from it. You can own it in File Cabinet No. 2, and pay tax on it when you withdraw money. Or you can own it in File Cabinet No. 3, where you will have already paid taxes on the cash before you put it in, and you can remove your cash tax free.

In a perfect world, there would be a File Cabinet No. 4, in which taxes would never come due—Uncle Sam would just go away and forget about filling his pockets. But if you remember how money grows—the eighteenth hole in the game of golf was worth $13,800—then you'll see that paying tax on the back end, particularly when you can't pin down the tax rate, can be a costly choice. Your better alternative is to pay the tax on the seed rather than on the harvest.

Throughout history, people have secured their futures by receiving tax-free income, often through tax-free municipal bonds, so that they could be certain how much income they would receive free from Uncle Sam. This allowed them to plan for their future lifestyles and not be burdened by the complexities of taxes in their later years. Today, the PPP works as the municipal bond once did. (Also, the new "Roth IRA" gives you some limited opportunity to grow your money tax free and take it out tax free.)

As the "variable" part of "flexible premium variable life insurance plan" implies, the returns from investments in the plan are variable, because the stock market can go up or down. The "flexible premium" part means that you can put different amounts into your plan in different years, if you choose to do so. The "life insurance" part refers to the term insurance that wraps the plan. As required by all insurance plans, you must show good health—part of your Wheel of Life—before you can set up the plan.

I discussed all of these factors with Betty so she would have a basic understanding of the PPP. But she was still skeptical about the tax-free nature of withdrawal.

"How do you do it? How does that work? I mean, it's a miracle to extricate anything tax free," she exclaimed.

The answer is easy. As far back as your great-grandmother, or even her mother, people owned insurance policies in which they had socked away some extra cash. If they needed money at some point, they could borrow against their policies—tax free. It's this ability to "borrow" money tax free against a life insurance policy that enables you to withdraw funds tax free from a PPP, because when you withdraw cash from your PPP, you are technically "borrowing" it against your insurance policy. But the major difference between the PPP and conventional life insurance policies is that if you borrow money against a traditional policy, you have to repay it. If you withdraw money from a PPP, you never have to repay it. Instead, "the net surrender value" of your policy is reduced by the amount you withdraw, as are the lump-sum death benefits to your heir or heirs.

"Joan, I am very taken by the PPP, and I'm definitely going to apply for one. But why haven't I heard about this before?" Betty asked.

"Not many brokerage firms and only a few insurance companies can tell you about this type of investment, because it takes expertise in both areas to create it," I said.

But the field is expanding rapidly. Investors are becoming aware that qualified plans aren't working as well as they once did. In response, brokerage firms are creating their own PPPs, and insurance companies are pairing with mutual funds to create them. The PPPs offered by each of these companies differ widely. You can evaluate three essential factors to make sure that you're choosing a good plan:

1. Is the borrowing rate to take money out of your private pension plan less than .5 percent, and is it guaranteed for life?
2. Do the mutual funds offered in the plan have a five-to-ten-year record of an annual average return of 12 percent or better?
3. Are the term insurance costs about the same as or lower than those of other plans?

If the answer to all three questions is yes, you're on the right track.

The beauty of File Cabinet No. 3 is that you can have a private pension plan even if you also have qualified plans in File Cabinet No. 2. So if, like Betty, you have a 401(k) plan, but you know that it's not going to produce enough cash for you, you can also have a PPP.

Also, the private pension plan belongs to you, not your employer. That means that when you change jobs or move across the country, your PPP goes with you. You own it, you are completely responsible for setting it up, funding it, deciding when you'll take cash out of it, and matching it to your lifestyle.

For example, let's say you're forty-five, and you have been funding a private pension plan since you were thirty-five. You decide to quit your job and take time off to travel for a while and work on that novel you have always yearned to write. So you stop contributing to your plan, take out some cash so you can live for a few years, finish writing your book, go back to work, and start putting money back into your PPP until you're sixty-five. The plan is that flexible.

You also do not report it on your tax return (you are not mandated by law to do so), so it is not apparent to Uncle Sam that you are accumulating this cash—and it might be substantial cash. Those who are concerned about financial privacy find this feature attractive.

If you have a domestic partner, the private pension plan solves the problem of how to leave your assets to him or her. In your PPP, name your partner as the beneficiary and, by law, she or he will receive the wealth from your plan tax free.

Again, setting up a private pension plan in our office entails filling out some forms, obtaining approval for insurance coverage—approval requires a medical review—and then setting up the investment account. It's your decision how you wish to pay into your plan. You may choose to have monthly deductions made from your paycheck, or you may simply write a check quarterly, semiannually or annually. Once you're in motion, just plug in the money and watch it grow.

Building Betty's Financial Plan

"I get the picture," Betty said. "Basically, my money is now grouped in choices from File Cabinet No. 2, which includes my IRA and my 401(k). My $10,000 is cash-in-waiting. And what about the cash that's in my insurance policy? Is that a private pension plan?"

"Not yet," I responded. "But it's a start."

What Betty has is the old type of insurance. Her father probably bought it for her for protection. By converting that old plan into a new form of insurance, it will continue to include protection coverage, but will primarily be an investment to grow money tax free. The big difference between the two types of insurance is that the cash in her old policy is earning money at a small interest rate, a rate that the insurance company established some time ago. The new form will invest her money in mutual funds in order to take advantage of growth in the stock market, and, as you now know, that makes a tremendous difference. This explains why insurance was never considered to be an investment. Today, though, it's a primary tool in the good growth of your money.

"Just as we can move an IRA from one location to another, we can move cash from your old insurance policy to a new one," I told Betty. "So this policy your father gave you could be the start of your new private pension plan. It could be a File Cabinet No. 3 stock drawer investment."

"Okay. Let me figure this out. I'm forty-two years old. If I assume my money will grow at a 12 percent rate of return, then according to the Rule of 72, it will double every six years. That means that, until I'm sixty-five, my money has the potential to double about four times," Betty pondered.

"I see where you're going," I said. "You want to know how much you'll have in your IRA and 401(k) plan by the time you're sixty-five, right?"

"Yep. I'm wondering what life will be like then," Betty said. "Let's see—$25,000 in my 401(k) plan and $5,000 in my IRA. That's $30,000 invested right now. So using that doubling rule, if my money doubles four times, then my $30,000 turns into $60,000, which turns into $120,000, and that turns into $240,000, then $480,000. Wow! I'm going to love watching that money grow."

"If, at age sixty-five, you have half a million in an investment that pays you 8 percent per year, your investment will give you an annual income of $40,000," I added.

"Yes. But remember, Joan. You said that Uncle Sam was going to want to collect his tax. So if I assume that combined federal and state taxes will be around 50 percent when I reach sixty-five, I'll actually have only $20,000 to spend each year. My problem is, that's not going to be enough for me to do the things I'll want to do at that time. But it's a start, and I'm glad I've done as much as I have, because at least with this, I realize I will be able to meet my essential needs—my dignity money. But the other thing that concerns me is that, in twenty-three years, $20,000 isn't going to have the same spending power as it does now. I need to do some more investing because I haven't built my Money Machine to where I want it to be," Betty concluded.

"And where do you want it to be?" I asked.

"Oh, somewhere in the neighborhood of $150,000 a year," Betty said.

"Well, that's a real nice neighborhood. But tell me: Is that $150,000 after taxes?"

"Why not?"

"Okay. Let's work this through," I offered. "If we take that $10,000 that's sitting on top of File Cabinet No. 1 and make a plan, you can get there. Can you also invest a new $10,000 each year from your earnings?"

"I should be able to. I make a good salary, and there are expenses I can readily cut out, like cab rides, extra clothes, and a few dinners and lunches here and there. And this is important to me, so I can figure out a way to create some side income."

"Well, I sure hope you aren't going to start working eighteen-hour days again to get that extra cash," I said.

"Oh, no," Betty replied. "I want to put some distance between me and my office. What I had in mind was selling my pottery to some of those little shops in the Bay Area, Santa Cruz, or right here in Los Gatos," she said. "The work would give me great pleasure."

"I think you'll have a ready market for your work—people around here just adore handcrafted items—plus you will be adding joy to your life," I said.

So this is what Betty did with the $10,000: She kept $2,500 in her checking account as a cushion, stashed $2,500 in a money market account for unusual expenses, and invested another $5,000 in the 401(k) plan offered by her employer. The most important reason for this last move is that her firm matches her contribution by depositing into her account 35 percent of what she puts in each month. A 30 percent or more match makes it worthwhile to use the 401(k). However, if your employer does not match your contribution, or if you are the employer and you have the additional cost of maintaining such a plan and funding it for your employees, then a 401(k) or other qualified plan makes a lot less sense.

Notice that Betty has made no additional contributions to her IRA. She's allowing the $5,000 she has invested in it to remain as is.

Next, Betty took the cash in her old insurance policy and some money from her salary and started a private pension plan. She's committed $10,000 a year to her plan; the money will come from her earnings. By investing through age sixty-four, and projecting an average annual return of 12 percent on her investments, she'll get good results from her PPP. We projected that she will create a cash flow for herself of about $89,600 a year, tax free, from age sixty-five until age eighty-five. Also, she'll have $633,831 in life insurance for protection right from the start.

The life insurance will also go to her beneficiary tax free, and this is useful in estate planning. If you plan to bequeath someone a piece of property, it's a good idea to also leave some insurance proceeds to them so they are not forced to sell the property in order to satisfy the IRS, which will demand an estate tax payment ninety days after the inheritance. Betty also committed to doing a will.

By this time, Betty was on a roll. "Let's see," she said, "I'll move the $25,000 in my 401(k) plan out of the bond drawer and into the stock drawer to best grow my money. Then, if I have $24,000 a year from my investments in File Cabinet No. 2 and $89,600 from my private pension plan in File Cabinet No. 3, I'll have about $113,600 to spend free of any taxes when I'm sixty-five and well into my nineties. It's not the $150,000 I set out to get, but I like it! Now I really want to live a long life."

Betty's Money Machine will be churning and burning, and she certainly won't be out working until she's seventy-five just so she can pay her bills.

Betty has successfully tackled her personal money matters. She can make a good estimate of the cash that will come from her Money Machine when she's ready to depend upon it. As she goes along and monitors the actual results from her investments, she'll continue to revise her projections. But now that she has this plan, she has only two jobs left. One is to invest regularly, and the other is to watch that her investments are growing on the average of 12 percent a year. And there's a third: to smile, knowing that she's handled this part of her Wheel of Life.

"Let's see. I pick the file cabinet depending upon how I want to be taxed, and I pick the wave of the future for my stock drawer. And then I stay planted, and try not to outsmart the market or get persuaded by hype. Is that it?" Betty asked.

"That's pretty much it," I responded. "And you'll build your Money Machine your own way for your future."

"I can't tell you how relieved I feel," Betty said. "For several months, I've had this terrible, edgy feeling. Now I'm feeling better, much better."

The lines in Betty's face had relaxed for the first time since I met her. Her skin had a glow, and she sparkled as much as the yellow tulips she had showered me with.

She left my office knowing the specifics of how she would derive

$113,600 a year from her Money Machine into her nineties. I suspected that with that sense of security, her entire Wheel of Life was going to roll along at a new and energized clip.

Building Other Money Machines

Let's see how the file cabinets work for other women.

June Mendoza, the Michigan housewife, called me one day with the sad news that her father had died. She was bereft with grief, of course, but she also faced the burden of helping to manage the assets her father had left for her seventy-three-year-old mother. These included $125,000 from a life insurance policy, $18,000 in stocks and bonds, a coin collection, and a small income from the pension plan her father's company had given him. June's father also left June an investment nest egg, although it was smaller than the one he had left her mother.

True to the pattern she had established—and accepted—in her marriage, June thought she could simply dump the responsibility of her father's estate on her husband, Steve. After all, he took care of all her financial needs; why shouldn't he also invest and direct her mother's cash?

Sure enough, when June sat down to talk to her husband about taking on financial duties for his mother-in-law, he readily agreed to do so. But then June asked him what he was going to do with the funds. His response: Put them in the bank!

"Joan, I have never before in my life questioned Steve's judgment with these things," she said. "But it just doesn't sit right with me. That seems like an awful lot of money to give a bank."

"You're right. There are much better choices," I offered.

"I don't know what to do. It's my mother, and I want the best for her," June said.

"I'm sure you do. But before we work out some strategies for your mother, tell me something, June. What is *your* money invested in?" I asked.

There was an embarrassed silence.

"I don't know," she finally replied.

"What if you were in your mother's situation today—if something were to happen to Steve? Where would you be financially? Do you have any idea what your financial future looks like?" I continued.

You could almost hear the thunder. June was aghast.

"I'm in trouble, aren't I? And I guess my mother is, too, if I don't do something," she said.

June had finally caught up with the revolution. She was ready to start the process of financial self-discovery. But I sensed that it would be best for me to pull back a bit and let June proceed at her own pace.

I encouraged her to sit down with Steve and find out what their money picture looked like. I also suggested that she figure out who would assume stewardship of her mother's inheritance, and that she give some thought to what strategies she'd like to explore. I gently pointed out to her that, at seventy-three, her mother could live another ten, fifteen, or even twenty years, and that she'd need income to cover that time and to pay for any medical needs or long-term care not covered by her insurance. Recalling the money she and Steve had shoveled out for various treatments for their daughter Ellie's eating disorder, June could relate to that. I urged her to take some time to sort through what we'd discussed.

June called me back at the end of the week. Her voice was crisp and businesslike, and I detected a strong note of self-assurance. Could this be the same woman who, at the Ranch, had shown so much disinterest in money matters?

Her mother's dilemma had galvanized her into action. She'd finally sat down with her husband to talk money. Steve works for a pharmaceutical firm, and he earns $55,000 a year, plus bonuses. They manage to pay their bills and indulge in some simple pleasures, but their financial margin is thin because of the cascade of cash that went to help their daughter and to educate all of their children. However, they do own a condo and a small cabin in the country, where they go on weekends to unwind.

June learned from her talks with Steve that he had never really aggressively invested any of their money because he never trusted brokers. What cash they had accumulated went into savings accounts or CDs with low yields. In short, Steve hadn't grown much cash. Because of their shared cultural mind-set, it never occurred to Steve to discuss finances with June. After all, Steve had always thought, "I'm the breadwinner—it's my right and my responsibility to take care of money matters. Why should I burden June?" And to the extent that June had thought about it, she'd agreed. But now her assumptions about male and female roles were changing.

June accepted some of the blame for the poor state of her family finances, but, more important, she realized there was a lot of work to do. First, she had her mother's money to think about. Then, she had her own nest egg to consider. June's father left her an investment portfolio worth $30,000, which has the potential to grow nicely.

My first question was, how protected was June? I asked her whether Steve had any life insurance policies.

"I really don't know, but I'll find out," she responded.

Steve needed insurance, I explained, to ensure that if he were gone, June would not suddenly be left without a home because she could not keep up the mortgage payments.

I also asked her about their country home. Could they really afford this second house in their current financial situation? Perhaps, I suggested, they were putting the cart before the horse by placing more priority on enjoying their summer vacations than on setting up their long-term financial futures. The house has potential value, I told June, because she and Steve could rent or sell it and add the cash to their Money Machine. But to build wealth they'd need to begin thinking about their cabin as a possible source of cash flow, not just a personal luxury.

June promised to talk to her husband about using the house to generate a little income. She also said they'd call me back—together—to discuss strategies for growing June's mother's cash, and that she would find out exactly what was in the stock portfolio her dad had bequeathed her.

After a lengthy discussion with Steve, June went through all the bank accounts and sent me copies so I could help her interpret them. She decided to close the bank accounts and to not renew the CDs when they mature. Instead, June and Steve will use the money to invest $15,000 a year in a private pension plan for Steve, who is forty-seven years old (three years younger than June).

Why create the plan for Steve and not June? June does not work and has no income; Steve does. Putting the PPP in Steve's name will give them both a steady income in his nonworking years and will provide June with protection in the event of his death. The cost of the term insurance portion is about $110 a month, or $1,320 a year. June and Steve will invest the balance, or $12,700, in mutual funds that they will select after she receives information about them from me. Their money will grow in these mutual funds until they're ready to use it.

There's no limitation, after the first year, on when they can withdraw money. But June and Steve plan not to touch the money. They want to leave it all in to grow, as in the game of golf, for their future. If we project that this money will grow at 12 percent per year, the stock market's historic rate of return, we see that Steve and June will have an annual tax-free income of about $70,000 from the time that Steve is sixty-five until he is eighty-five. They'll have a stream of income, driven by the engine of the stock market and protected from taxation by the insurance in their PPP and insurance protection.

Linette Atwood also plans to contribute $10,000 a year to a PPP. She's now thirty-eight, so her money has more time to grow than Betty's or Steve and June's. Assuming her investments will earn a 12 percent average rate of return, Linette projects that she'll have an annual tax-free income of $137,000 from age sixty-five to age eighty-five. Plus, she'll be able to tap into her PPP's cash before she is sixty-five if she needs to help pay for her daughter's college education. She'll also set up an education IRA for her daughter.

You can look to your PPP as the sole source of your future income, or you can combine the income from a PPP with the income from a qualified plan, such as an IRA.

What About an Annuity?

If you've been investigating your financial options, you may have heard about annuities, an investment choice I haven't mentioned until now. But if you have never really understood what an annuity is, don't worry—you can scratch it off your list of possible investments. An annuity isn't a wealth-building strategy. The marketing line for annuities is that they shelter investments from taxation. They do, but not effectively, because an annuity protects your money in only one out of three cases. Annuities protect only the growth of investments. If you invest in an annuity, you won't get a deduction when you put your money in as you do if you invest in an IRA. And you won't be able to withdraw your money tax free as you can from a private pension plan. When you withdraw money from an annuity, you pay the regular income tax instead of the capital gains tax. Also, an annuity, like a qualified plan, ties up your money until you are fifty-nine and a half.

As you can see, annuities are not a great investment option. By the time you pay annuity charges, annual expenses, and income tax on the money you withdraw, it could take from ten to fifteen years to earn more than you would have if you had chosen a similar investment in File Cabinet No. 1.

One more thing about annuities that really raises my hackles. Sometimes, I see a broker invest someone's money that's in an IRA in an annuity. This makes no sense. After all, like any qualified plan, an IRA already shelters the growth of investment income from taxes, so why would you need to pay additional charges to have an annuity shelter it as well? That's what I call malpractice, and investing in an annuity that's already inside an IRA is clearly not a strategy for a Money Machine.

If you own an annuity, make a point to find out how it's performing—maybe some of its mutual funds are doing better than others. If your annuity is inside your IRA, check to see how much it would cost to get out of it, and then continue to invest the money in your IRA.

SIMPLIFYING YOUR INVESTMENTS

Let's consider the woman whose investments read like a road map of the world. Intent on financial security, and perhaps overly mindful of the value of diversification, she has invested in many different things, but now she has become frustrated because her investments all seem like such a jumble, and managing them is so time consuming.

That's the case with Sadie Chung, the petite fifty-nine-year-old poet and author we met at the Ranch in Mexico. Over the years, she's accumulated three IRAs—one in a bank and two at different brokerage firms. She also has investments in her former employer's company pension plan, an annuity her late husband purchased for her, stocks in an account at one brokerage firm, and bonds in an account at another brokerage firm. Her husband also left her a batch of individual stocks and mutual funds, $750,000 in cash from his life insurance policy, some commercial property in Hong Kong, and a condo on Fisher Island in Miami. She invested in a limited partnership, and she recently set up her own company and a company-sponsored retirement plan. And with all that, she still finds time to work part-time as a poet and lecturer in creative writing.

"How does this all add up in my Money Machine? Remember, my broker made me sell my mutual funds and move to bonds. How do I know what to do?" she asked in utter frustration.

For Sadie, I immediately prescribed the KISS theory: "Keep It Sleek and Simple!" Sadie is out of control—or at least her investments are. She's buried under a mountain of financial statements, which give her lots of information presented in ways she can't decipher; she'd have to take courses in accounting, investing, economics, and law to figure it all out.

Sadie will have to do some major reorganization before she can clearly see what all her investments will mean to her financial future. And while she's out of control, she might be missing a good investment opportunity because she's relying on someone else's judgment rather then her own.

Here's how Sadie's money management can be simplified. For starters, her three IRA accounts can be rolled together into one IRA. Two securities accounts can be rolled into one. And the pension money from her former employer can be rolled into her new IRA account. These steps require only a few phone calls and a form or two, and they take Sadie from six statements to two—one for her IRA account and one for her regular brokerage account. Next, she can look inside each account and see what's in them and whether the investments are performing well. She can also diversify within each account by investing in different stocks, types of funds, and mutual fund families.

Turning to Sadie's annuity, I noticed that it was held by a major bank. But it didn't look very good to me. It appeared that the annuity had a guaranteed rate of 5 percent until an anniversary date. We looked a little further, and I suggested to Sadie that she call the bank and obtain more specific information. She found out that, yes, the 5 percent rate was guaranteed until the end of the month; then the rate would drop to 3 percent!

We were astounded. Three into 72 meant that it would take twenty-four years for her money to double! That same year—1995—was an exceptional one for the stock market, with mutual funds that returned 35 percent. Clearly, the bank, not Sadie, was benefiting from Sadie's annuity. The bank was taking Sadie's money, investing it in the stock market, paying Sadie her 5 percent return, and pocketing the difference! We made a quick decision to roll right out of that annuity and into another one that allowed her to benefit from the higher returns of the stock market.

It is important to simplify your financial life wherever possible so that you can fully understand and take charge of what you have. If an investment is too complex for you to manage, don't buy it. Simplifying your holdings will make it easy to determine how much cash your investments will pay you in the future so you can monitor the growth of your Money Machine.

By taking control of her financial life, Sadie is well positioned to be financially free. When her investment picture looked like a spilled jigsaw puzzle, she was frustrated; she even considered quitting all other pursuits to deal with her financial life full-time. Now she has some peace of mind. She is enjoying building her financial future, even while she continues the other areas in her life that mean so much to her.

Sadie's so excited about her Money Machine that she's teaching its principles to her nieces. Erica and Danielle came to my office with baby-sitting money in hand, and we've set up two brokerage accounts for them. Both girls have been tickled to watch their Money Machines grow.

Danielle was so excited that she told a sixteen-year-old friend, Karen, to come see me so that she, too, could start a Money Machine. Karen visited me, and we talked about growing money, the game of golf, the Rule of 72, and the many years Karen has to develop her financial resources.

When I was finished, the young woman said: "I have to tell you that my parents advised me not to see you. They said that to invest money, you have to pay too many commissions and stuff. But I just wanted to tell you that I've learned a lot. Thanks."

That I might have opened up her thinking was all the thanks I needed.

It's wonderful how taking on life's challenges truly strengthens us. The results can be positively joyful. That's what I see in the faces of women—like you!—who are taking charge of their financial lives.

10

Choosing an Advocate:
Brokers, Advisers, and
Financial Planners

Shopping for an Advocate
Being an Informed Investor
Types of Financial Advocates
What to Do When You Get the Runaround

hen it comes to choosing the right coach to guide you and help you look after your investments, the best advocate you can find is *you*.

Maybe you're wondering what special gifts you can bring to the investment table. Well, you'd be surprised. To begin with, by having read this far, you've already examined your lifestyle, your spending plan, and your income, and you've thought long and hard about your relationship to money—how it has helped you and how it may have hindered you. Furthermore, you've thought about how you want to live in the future and what types of investments you'll need in your Money Machine. In short, you—more than anyone else—know the realities of your present and future situation. And after reading the preceding chapters, you understand what your investment options are and which ones will best nourish the lifestyle you desire.

You still may not know everything you need to know in order to make your Money Machine run silky smooth, but you know enough to recognize the things that work and those that don't—and to set some standards. You'll need to hold yourself accountable for the results, too, and be flexible and nurturing when one approach or another doesn't satisfy your goal. That's something we intuitively and instinctively know as women, and that's the simple beauty of it. It does take courage to build a financial future, but if you don't actively participate, you'll be off to a false start—you'll be heading *east* looking for a sunset!

On the other hand, if you jump right in and take an active role, you'll be the best advocate you've ever had. Using the intuition you were born with, your knowledge of yourself and your dreams, and your growing understanding of how money works, you'll be positioned to structure your financial future. You'll know how to choose some good stocks or mutual funds, how to regularly invest in them, and how to monitor the results to determine how well your money is growing. You'll be able to measure your financial growth just as you are able to measure and encourage the growth of, say, your children or business. You'll be your best advocate.

Notice that I've been using the word "advocate." It's an unusual word in the investment world—you don't often hear brokers or advisers referred to as "advocates" for their clients. When I worked on Wall Street, I encountered brokers and so-called advisers who were caught up in a highly competitive and adversarial spin. It was "may the best man win," as if they were slamming through a game of hockey—using your money as the puck skidding across the ice. I heard brokers intentionally give misinformation, push investments for purposes other than the client's best interest, deliberately confuse clients in order to maintain control over their money, and work for their own self-interest far above anyone else's. This is not the behavior of an honest advocate, nor of anyone you would want to plug into one of those important spokes in your Wheel of Life.

Your financial life is not a game, and the idea isn't to align yourself with someone whose objective is to make more cash than the gal or guy at the next desk. As a consumer, you want and deserve something better. Many women—and men, too—have smartly avoided the brokerage and financial community because its typical way of doing business just doesn't feel right. That means we turn elsewhere. One approach is to try to eliminate middlemen, such as brokers, and to handle all investment decisions, even the details of buying and selling investments, on your own.

Not so long ago, this was virtually impossible, but the information revolution is changing that picture. As we discussed in Chapter 7, some of the on-line computer services offer you the opportunity to "sign on," open a brokerage account, and get started with your investments—with only a few strokes on the keyboard. Also, some companies offer no-load stocks or mutual funds. This allows individual investors, like you, to buy shares directly from the issuing company. This means you don't have to use an outside broker or pay any fees for the trade. Going directly to the company—Exxon, Mobil, and Kerr-McGee (a natural resources enterprise) are among the corporations that offer no-load stocks—cuts out the middleman.

Many investors feel, however, that they need more direction. If you want advice and investment ideas, or want simply to obtain better results than you are getting on your own, then it's time to choose an advocate.

What do you want in an advocate? Very simply, a person who works with you to develop the best possible strategies for your personal financial needs; you want someone who gets results that build your Money Machine. This advocate may be a broker or financial adviser who has achieved measurable results on her or his own. Underline *measurable* results, because you don't want to adopt the strategies and beliefs of someone who is also heading east looking for a sunset! You want to select an advocate who is mature and responsible for her or his own financial well-being, because this individual will essentially be applying the same approach on your behalf.

The aim is to find someone who can work with you. Finding the right financial advocate can be very much like finding the perfect personal trainer—someone who is compassionate and courteous, someone you can respect because she or he is knowledgeable, someone who has standards and strategies you can embrace. Equally important, you want a person who looks out for your growth and development. You don't want someone who is just around to collect her or his fee for a workout session. In short, you want someone who will champion your cause and do everything possible—including expanding her or his knowledge—to advance your financial goals.

Although you may create and manage your Money Machine on your own, in my experience, an essential key to jump-starting your Money Machine is to partner with an advocate. You won't turn over your money to this person without understanding and agreeing with her or his financial advice, any more than you'd turn over your body to a physician without understanding and agreeing with the doctor's diagnosis and recommendations. But you can greatly benefit from having an advocate who knows the investment world, who regularly tracks the investment markets, who acknowledges your goals, and who helps you develop realistic plans for achieving them.

As in any partnership, you'll reap more success with someone with whom you can easily communicate. Above all, you must choose an advocate who listens to you and whom you can trust. I'm not talking about someone who *tells* you that you can trust her or him—we've all heard the "lie down, I think I love you" line from the guy who's on the make! I mean someone who *demonstrates* that she or he is trustworthy. Always keep in mind: The financial results you achieve are not going to be your advocate's results. They're going to be *your* results—your financial future.

SHOPPING FOR AN ADVOCATE

Unfortunately, because there are unscrupulous brokers, financial firms whose policies are designed to protect the company rather than the investor, and financial advisers whose recommendations are ill informed and sometimes self-serving, looking for a good financial advocate can be like tiptoeing through a minefield. Here is a road map with some important benchmarks that can help get you safely through:

• Before you begin your search, ask for referrals from friends and associates you respect. Look for specific examples about how the person they recommend has been a good coach. This way, you'll avoid being referred to an adviser who is simply someone's brother, tennis buddy, or bowling partner.

• Evaluate your adviser using the same criteria you'd use in any other personal or professional relationship: Do you feel this person is honest, open, and accessible? Can you communicate easily with each other? If you dread calling your adviser because you're uncomfortable talking with her or him, some crucial conversations may never take place—and that can cost you money.

• Take time to shop around. You wouldn't buy the first house you see from the first real estate broker you visit; you probably wouldn't buy the first tomato you see when you shop at the market! Choose an advocate the same way. It never hurts to take another look to see who else is waiting to work with you.

• When you find someone you're interested in, be bold: Ask the person directly whether she or he will be working in your best interest. Then check in with your stomach in order to see whether you get a good feeling about the response. What's this person's mission or agenda? Everyone has one.

• You want someone who will help you track the growth of your Money Machine. Ask whether she or he will review your investment progress with you about every three months in order to help you assess any changes that need to be made.

• Ask for information that will help you evaluate whether your prospective advocate is nurturing the growth of her or his own financial well-being. Is she or he in or out of balance financially?

• Make sure your prospective advocate follows her or his own financial advice. You can determine this by directly asking your prospective advocate about her or his personal investments. You can also ask the firm for a history of the investments she or he has championed over the past few years and their track record.

• Even if you have a good feeling about someone, check out that person's track record within the industry. Approach it the way you'd approach a doctor's recommendation for minor surgery: Not only would you get a second, and sometimes a third opinion, but you also might call your state medical board to make sure you don't get a doctor who will cut off your foot if all you need is a nose job. To check out a broker, call the National Association of Securities Dealers (1-800-289-9999) and find out whether any complaints have been made against the person you have in mind. The NASD is a self-regulatory organization that encompasses all of the securities brokers in the United States. A call to the North American Securities Administrators Association (1-202-737-0990) will put you in touch with your state regulator, who can tell you whether a securities broker or financial adviser has been subject to any disciplinary action. Also, for a small fee, the Securities and Exchange Commission in Washington, D.C., will give a complete history of the business practices of anyone involved in the investment community.

• Ask whether the adviser's firm is covered by the Securities Investor Protection Corporation, which provides insurance against a broker's or a firm's failure.

• Run, don't walk, from any broker you've never met who calls you at home or in your office to sell you something. Like any other telephone solicitation, these "cold calls" are a hotbed of fraud and consumer abuse. Don't bite!

• Explore your prospective advocate's investment perspective to see whether it matches your beliefs. For example, you will probably not want someone who will want to trade the securities in your portfolio often, because you plan to be a long-term investor. And you want someone who is focused on the stock market—not bonds—because, as you've seen, stocks are the best way to build your wealth.

- Avoid any broker or adviser who appears condescending or disrespectful. To this day, Wall Street is filled with brokers who maintain stereotypes about women and money. Don't use a broker who acts as if he "knows better" what sort of investments are right for you, or one who tries to steer you toward investments that "women like."

- Above all, you don't want someone who tries to incite you into the "fear and greed" syndrome—someone who tells you what's hot so you buy it, and then talks you into selling it when it "cools off." This approach will only lead you to make out-of-balance and costly decisions. You'll want to sidestep that giant stomachache.

Once you know whom you want to consider, you're ready to interview your potential adviser to see whether this is a person with character and integrity with whom you can work and have a productive professional relationship. It's better to have this talk face-to-face rather than over the phone, if possible. This allows more intimacy, and it permits you to monitor more easily how someone is responding to you. Also, face-to-face meetings often reveal more about someone's personality, professional style, and point of view. And always remember, trust your gut. Whatever feeling you get in your belly about your prospective advocate is a true feeling, and it will signal how you will feel about working with this person into the future.

Before my first marriage, I forgot to ask the important, intimate questions about my fiancé's deep-seated values, dreams, and desires. I was much more concerned about superficial considerations: how physically attractive he was, whether or not he went to an Ivy League school, and whether he came from a "good" family. I learned the hard way that the more intimate questions were the important ones, and because I'd failed to probe them before entering deeply into a relationship, I suffered needlessly.

The same is true when you consider a relationship with a financial advocate. Less important is whether she or he works for one of the Big Five brokerage houses, or whether her or his office has

$50,000 worth of carpeting, $100,000 paintings hanging on the wall, and a $20,000 desk adorned with rare stone sculptures from China. Nor does it matter whether your adviser has a Harvard, Stanford, or Northwestern University MBA. Most important are the intimate details that reveal whether this person will have a good one-on-one relationship with you.

BEING AN INFORMED INVESTOR

Once you've connected with someone to handle your investments, you don't want to be a forgotten soul. That means you need to know what sort of contact you can expect from your advocate, and how available she or he will be to you. Will your advocate pick up the phone when you call or call you back within a reasonable amount of time? If not, will she or he have an assistant who will be fully familiar with your situation, and who will be available for you to talk to? Ask these questions before you finally choose an advocate. Better yet, call your advocate's office several times to see for yourself what kind of response you get.

Clear, frequent written communication is equally important if you are to be an informed investor. How often will your advocate send you an update of your account activities? If you don't understand something on your statement, or if you need more information, will your advocate readily supply it? And will that statement be easy to read and understand?

I've seen statements of accounts from various firms that even someone with an MBA and lots of years in the investment business can't decipher. Being comfortable with the information on statements that you receive from your advocate is fundamental. If you can't read them, you can't know how your money is doing. You'll want to be certain that your advocate will fully explain this information and other technical jargon and machinations of the investment world in language that doesn't intimidate or patronize you.

Here's an example of the type of letter we at Take Charge Financial! periodically send out to our clients:

Dear Investor:

Enclosed is your report for the third quarter of 1997. Keep it for reference, and if something looks other than what you expected, or if you have questions, let us know.

The enclosed report is an appraisal of the holdings you have in an account, or accounts, with us, and it tells you both what you paid for various securities and what they are worth as of September 30. This is the standard report that we send you each quarter so that you can see your "Money Machine" in progress. Next quarter, we will send you tax information so that you can see how income or the sale of securities will affect your taxes.

Most notable about this year so far in the market is that we continue to see the stock market trend upward—with some hiccups. I've enclosed a couple of charts to lend some perspective to viewing the stock market and its potential for you and me.

The first chart, from Ibbotson Associates (a firm that analyzes market information), shows the performance of the stock market from 1925 to 1996. The chart shows that in this period, small cap stocks have grown the best. Following in performance are international stocks and blue-chip stocks. The chart indicates that inflation and U.S. Treasury notes have grown more slowly than the three stock groups. This is a graphic display of the major growth that has occurred in the market—and the small blips that occasionally occur in its relentless upward movement.

The second page, also from Ibbotson, shows the "odds," so to speak, of investing in the market. Not bad odds, huh? You have a one-in-two chance of getting better than a 15 percent annual return from the market.

The third page is a chart that shows how you can profit when the market has one of its "liquidation sales": buy stocks on sale and reap the benefits. While the market has dipped occasionally, it has returned to a steady climb. You'll see in the comparison that if you consistently buy on sale (the bottom line on the graph), you will do better overall than if you buy regularly in an upward market. This chart illustrates a 20 percent return in the steady market, but an 86 percent return in the downward dipping market. And note that the bottom line ends below where it started.

In conclusion:

—Don't get too concerned about dips in the market. Pessimism mostly pays those who dispense it!

—Expect the market to dip—but a dip is only a blip on the screen of true opportunity. There's not a better place to be.

—Take advantage of dips as opportunities to add to your "Money Machine" at "on sale" prices.

Call us if you have any questions.

I hope this letter finds you making contributions to your world and enjoying every minute of it.

Live joyfully,

Joan Perry

P.S. You can send us checks periodically to deposit in your account, and money sitting uninvested will earn 4.25 percent in your money market account until you are ready to do something else with it.

This letter accompanies the Unrealized Gains and Losses report on page 196, which shows an example of an investment record. An investment record indicates the purchase date of the securities in this account, their purchase price, and their current value as of the statement date. Your entire investment history is before you, so you don't have to shuffle through files to figure out where you've been and where you are now.

You also want to know how your advocate keeps up with the ever-changing investment world. What does she or he do to remain current about the financial industry and to stay on top of the cutting-edge approaches to growing your money? When you ask about this, you'll want a response that shows you that this person is doing more than just selling the particular products that her or his firm promotes. (You can be sure that the firm will promote the products that are most lucrative for it to sell. After all, it is a business.) Your

Take Charge Financial!

UNREALIZED GAINS AND LOSSES

Zelda Ballow

September 30, 1997

DATE	QUANTITY	SECURITY	(Less Reinvested Divs.) UNIT COST	TOTAL COST	PRICE	MARKET VALUE	UNREALIZED GAIN/LOSS	% G/L
MUTUAL FUNDS								
07-31-95	1,110.15	GT Global Consumer Prod/Ser Fund, B Shares	13.39	14,865	22.37	24,834	9,969	67.1
01-07-97	250.00	GT Global Health Care Fund, B Shares	24.61	6,152	27.91	6,977	825	13.4
06-14-95	300.00	New Perspective Fund, Inc.	17.40	5,220	21.86	6,558	1,338	25.6
08-15-97	102.00	Oppenheimer Quest Value Fund, Class B	19.75	2,014	20.47	2,088	73	3.6
04-10-96	932.41	Putnam Fund for Growth & Income, Class A	17.32	16,149	21.91	20,429	4,280	26.5
06-14-95	200.00	Washington Mutual Investors Fund, Inc.	23.19	4,638	30.69	6,138	1,500	32.3
				49,039		67,025	17,986	36.7
COMMON STOCK								
06-15-95	200.00	Applied Materials, Inc.	41.50	8,300	95.25	19,050	10,750	129.5
06-15-95	400.00	Cisco Systems, Inc.	24.22	9,687	73.06	29,225	19,537	201.7
12-29-95	800.00	Dell Computer	8.66	6,925	96.87	77,500	70,575	1,019.1
06-15-95	200.00	Ford	29.62	5,925	45.12	9,025	3,100	52.3
06-15-95	200.00	Hewlett Packard	36.31	7,262	69.56	13,912	6,650	91.6
06-15-95	400.00	Intel Corp.	28.78	11,512	92.31	36,925	25,412	22.7
11-15-96	200.00	International Business Machines	72.50	14,500	106.00	21,200	6,700	46.2
09-27-96	100.00	Lucent Technology, Inc.	43.62	4,362	81.37	8,137	3,775	86.5
09-27-96	100.00	MMI Cos, Inc.	30.12	3,012	26.37	2,637	−375	−12.4
06-15-95	100.00	Microsoft Corp.	84.87	8,487	132.31	13,231	4,744	55.9
01-23-96	200.00	Red Brick Systems, Inc.	18.00	3,600	8.50	1,700	−1,900	−52.8
				83,575		232,544	148,969	178.2
TOTAL PORTFOLIO				132,614		299,568	166,954	125.9

The information in this report is provided but not guaranteed. "Unit Cost" is the purchase cost if acquired with TCF! or given to us by you, otherwise it is the cost the day it was transferred to TCF!.

advocate should be there to work on your behalf, to talk to you about investments that personally suit you, and to effectively serve you. To do this, your advocate must continually educate herself or himself.

TYPES OF FINANCIAL ADVOCATES

As you seek an advocate, you'll run across professionals who call themselves by a variety of names: brokers, financial planners, financial advisers, accountants. What do these different terms mean?

One major distinction is how your advocate gets paid. In the investment industry, compensation takes essentially one of two forms. A broker will receive a commission when you invest, say, in stocks or mutual funds. A financial adviser, on the other hand, will charge a fee, usually from around 1 to 1½ percent each year, on the total money in your account. Alternately, a planner may charge a flat hourly fee to help you set up your investment plan.

No one approach has a clear advantage. The choice is up to you, and what you decide will be based on your personal preference. However, it's useful to know in advance how your advocate gets paid.

A financial adviser can initiate a purchase or a sale of securities only by going through a broker. A broker, however, has direct access to the trading floor of the various exchanges and the over-the-counter market. This means that a broker can offer you more immediate trades. Both brokers and financial advisers must be licensed by the NASD. Both can help you develop an overview of your money life, and both can offer suggestions for making it work better and for reaching your financial goals. They can also help you decide what to do with a portion of your income, money you suddenly find yourself holding, or an inheritance, or help you figure out how to finance your children's education or get started in your money life.

These professionals often hold graduate degrees. Many also have additional certification. For example, a financial adviser may be a Certified Financial Planner (CFP), a designation awarded by the College of Financial Planning. A financial planner with more extensive training may be a Personal Financial Specialist (PFS) or a Chartered Financial Consultant (ChFC).

If you're looking for a planner, you can call the International Association for Financial Planning in Atlanta, Georgia (1-800-945-4237), to receive a list of referrals in your area.

Some accountants have the expertise to be helpful financial advocates. However, not all accountants are knowledgeable about investment strategies, the workings of the stock market, and other topics necessary for building a powerful Money Machine. An accountant may be necessary, however, if your personal or business finances become so complicated that managing your records and paying your taxes are complex and burdensome. Besides having academic degrees in accounting, an accountant should be certified by the American Institute of Certified Public Accountants. Some accountants, especially tax accountants, even have law degrees.

WHAT TO DO WHEN YOU GET THE RUNAROUND

Sometimes, when women sit down to talk to prospective advocates, they can't even get to first base. When I was at the Ranch, Sadie Chung told a whopping story about how she tried to get a broker to handle her money.

After her husband died, Sadie was a woman with a mission. She had $100,000 she wanted to invest. She had never invested on her own, and, like many women of her generation, she had left financial planning to her husband. Now she would have to take charge herself. After initially using her husband's broker, who switched all her mutual fund investment into bonds, Sadie sought referrals for other brokers. She asked her lawyer, who she thought would be able to give her a reliable recommendation. He referred her to a man—let's call him Charlie—who had been his broker for a decade. Charlie worked for one of the largest firms on Wall Street.

Sadie made an appointment. She thought all she had to do was walk in, present her money, have Charlie explain her investments, sign some papers, and go back home, secure in the knowledge that a trusted advocate was growing her money. As it turned out, this was not the case.

"Charlie took my cash, put it in a money market account, and never got back to me about what kind of investments I should make with it," Sadie said. "When I called him, he was always too busy to talk to me."

Then she went to Bob, who dismissed Sadie and asked to see her husband.

Charlie and Bob don't typify the industry, but attitudes like theirs can cripple investors and give the business a bad name. Like all too many brokers, Charlie and Bob assumed that men are more likely to earn an income and be the more active—that is profitable—brokerage client. Besides, the Charlies and Bobs of the world believe that men, unlike women, know how to make snap decisions and so need less attention in the long run.

The sort of discrimination Sadie experienced exists throughout the financial community. When I sought my first business loan in order to set up my first company, every major bank in Philadelphia turned me down. Yet I had $200,000 in municipal bonds as collateral, and male applicants showing up with a lot less than I had no problem securing loans. What happened to me is similar to what happens to many minority-owned businesses. Ironically, I finally did get a loan—from a minority-owned bank.

I was fortunate, and ultimately so was Sadie. As you saw in an earlier chapter, she sorted out her investments, and she is doing just fine. But some women encounter slick advisers who appear well meaning. Such advisers are not really their clients' advocates.

Let's stop here. Whether you've just taken the first steps to establish a relationship with an advocate, or whether you've been working with someone for decades, if you have an uneasy feeling in your stomach about how it's all working, take notice. Remember the old Paul Simon song? "There must be fifty ways to leave your lover [broker/financial adviser] . . . Make a new plan, Stan [Suzanne] . . . Get a new ploy, Roy [Joy] . . . Just get yourself free." In other words, you can always move on to someone else.

It's easy to move your financial accounts from one firm to another. You don't even have to talk to your former advocate—who may have turned out not to be an advocate at all—unless you want to do so as a courtesy. In our office, we give clients who come to us from other brokers a "transfer form." The client, who owns securities in another account, signs the form. Then we take care to make sure that all of the client's assets are transferred into a new account set up for her through our office. It might take three weeks or so to complete the transfer. Any investment firm can do this for its clients. It's a lot easier than a divorce!

So don't dummy up over a money partnership that isn't working. Your participation, and therefore your results, depend upon a quality relationship with your advocate. Expect no less.

You'll sense you're working with the wrong person if you have an experience like one I once had. This was a decade or so ago, when I was experimenting with ways to grow money and dabbling in investments other than stocks listed on the stock exchange. I turned to someone I thought had more skill than I—an investment professional who said, "You own some conservative stock. You ought to have something that's going to grow a lot more." He suggested that I invest in a project in which I could lose all my money. "This is going to be the hottest company of the eighties and possibly the nineties," he rhapsodized. It was a company that made plastic boxes for children's toys, paint supplies, and play cosmetics; it was a legitimate firm that even sold its little containers to Toys "R" Us. So I liberated $25,000 from my checking account for a project that I thought would certainly make my Money Machine purr like the engine of a Rolls-Royce Silver Shadow.

I bet you can guess the outcome. I haven't made a dime off that company, and I never got my money back.

I ditched that adviser faster than I could say "plastic box," and I went on to trust the stock market as a steady and proven wealth builder.

Before coming to me as a client, Rachel had problems with the financial advice her broker had been giving her. She and her husband, David, wanted to take $3,500 from their money market account and invest the money in a mutual fund. But Rachel's broker told her to stay put.

"I feel like I'm swimming through syrup," she told me. "I'm watching my friends build money on the stock market, and I'm not moving at all."

Rachel asked her adviser why he hadn't taken $3,500 from their money market account and put the money into a mutual fund as she and her husband had requested. He told her she didn't have enough cash, as he put it, "to play in the major league." That, of course, is nonsense. Many investors are small investors. According to a study by the New York Stock Exchange, 40 percent of those who invest in the stock market have annual incomes of under $25,000. So the $1,000 or $5,000 that you are growing in your account is just as important as someone else's $50,000 or $100,000. Don't let any broker tell you otherwise.

In any case, wealthy investors face the same challenges with their brokers and financial advisers as small investors do. A 1995 survey conducted by the Institute for Private Investors found that most millionaires had complaints about the relationships that they had formed; sixty-two percent of the millionaires surveyed said that they had changed their broker or financial adviser.

Rachel didn't realize she could leave her broker without any penalties or fees. As soon as she knew she could, she did. She chose to invest her money in a mutual fund, which gave her a good return—far better than she'd been receiving in her money market fund—and she got on with her financial life.

Always remember, you must be comfortable with your advocate on every level: You both must have open, clear communication; she or he must have expert knowledge and excellent interpersonal skills.

And you must be satisfied with the progress of your investments. You'll be in good shape if you

1. Establish a quality relationship with your advocate;
2. Believe in the investment choices you've made; and
3. Review what's in your Money Machine each quarter to see that it's growing.

Of course, your advocate is not a magician. Your advocate can't make you an instant millionaire any more than a personal trainer can wave a wand and give you a perfectly shaped, perfectly toned body. Yet you want to be sure that your investments are growing at an acceptable rate.

How will you know whether your investments are on track?

As you review your Money Machine each quarter, expect to track the overall market with your investments. Sometimes, the stock market will decline—that is, the market will have a periodic liquidation sale—and other times, it will rise, and the stock market will make rapid gains. If your results are close to the overall movement of the Dow, then you're in good shape. For example, if the Dow moved up from 5,500 to 5,690 in the quarter, you could expect to see a similar rise of 3 percent in the value of your own investments. Similarly, if the Dow moved downward from 5,500 to 5,390, you might see a decline of 2 percent in the value of your stocks. If you are losing ground to the Dow for two or more quarters in succession, then something may need some fine-tuning. Perhaps it is time to reevaluate your choices—either your choice of investments or your choice of advocate. Because your advocate should be working with you to gain the best of what the stock market has to offer, no less and no more.

This comparison of your portfolio's performance to that of the Dow will at least be a useful starting point for discussing your investments with your advocate. There may be a good reason that your portfolio lags the Dow for a time. For example, your investments may be weighted with international stocks, whose performance can be expected to differ from that of U.S. stocks. If you have solid reasons for believing that international stocks continue to be a good investment, you may want to temporarily accept slower growth in expectation of long-term gains. Or perhaps you have significant investments in high-tech industries, like computer software companies. These usually outperform the Dow when they're in favor and do worse than the overall market when they are out of favor. Again, they may be good investments despite their ups and downs. Discussing these details with your advocate will broaden your understanding of the investment potential of your Money Machine.

As you saw in the sample Unrealized Gains and Losses report on page 196, our company designed a system to track the quarterly performance of each of our clients' portfolios. You can do the same thing by using a small spreadsheet. Record the number of shares of a stock or mutual fund that you purchased, the purchase price, and the purchase date. Then at the end of each quarter, get the closing price of each of your stocks or mutual funds and plug that into the next column of your spreadsheet. (You can get the prices from the financial section of your newspaper, through your favorite on-line service, or from a web page of a national exchange, like NASDAQ, on the Internet. The NASDAQ website at www.NASDAQ.com has a spreadsheet that allows you to input your portfolio and regularly update the prices of your holdings.) Or some simple math will let you know whether you are growing your investment.

If you have a 401(k) plan, another type of company pension plan, an annuity, or a private pension plan, the same process applies. Of course, your advocate may have her or his version of a quarterly performance review. One way or another, you're in good shape when you can periodically review your investments.

Make sure that you have authorized every move in your account. If your statement lists a trade or change you know nothing about, talk to your advocate. It might be an error, and it can be rectified easily and quickly. If you suspect something else, then talk to the office manager at your brokerage house or adviser. If you are still troubled, then take your problem to the SEC or the NASD. There is also the National Council of Individual Investors, a new advocacy group for small investors. Based in Washington, D.C., it was set up by a group of securities officials from various states.

Getting good results while maintaining a trustworthy and open partnership is a primary goal of the advocate, whether that advocate is you or someone else.

11

Investing with a Partner: Mates, Friends, and Investment Clubs

Partnering with Your Mate or Friend

Partnering with an Investment Club

Over the past few decades, many women have reassessed their approach to relationships. Women have gained new degrees of self-reliance they rarely enjoyed before, and some have taken advantage of this freedom to dramatically change their lives—sometimes by ending old relationships that were one-sided or abusive and starting new ones on terms that worked better for them. Through it all, one thing has been clear: Being self-reliant never meant being celibate! Instead, it suggests that women (and men) improve their partnership skills, and take responsibility for negotiating and maintaining mutually satisfying unions.

The same philosophy applies to a woman's financial self-reliance. Freeing yourself from the White Knight Syndrome and taking full responsibility for your financial future, doesn't mean that you shy away from investing with a partner—whether the partner is a spouse, a lover, or a friend. I'm advocating only that you do so with knowledge and confidence in your own competence and sense of being. Investing with a husband, domestic partner, friend, or family member requires that you maintain your sense of self while you enjoy the benefits of the relationship.

This chapter offers you a chance to look at investing with a partner through fresh eyes. Because we finally have the tools to make independent decisions, women now have the opportunity to enter into truly egalitarian financial partnerships in which they share responsibility and make joint decisions with comfort and style.

And whether you're investing on your own or with someone else, just remember: It's still *your* financial future, and that future will be the consequence of decisions you and your partner or partners make. You're not alone in this, and whatever action you take also affects the financial health of someone else. Your partner is putting trust for the quality of his or her life into your hands by agreeing to invest with you.

Women have opened their lives to partners as a way to learn, to grow, to share themselves, and to experience with someone else the ups and downs of life. Choosing to partner in the money area of life offers many of the same benefits that are enjoyed in other areas. Investing with a partner can be enriching in every way—it can be great for the relationship and great for the Money Machine. But the temptation to give up your personal responsibility for your future is always lurking in any such partnership, and the process itself may have moments of challenge and frustration. At times, this partnership will require your absolute patience and conviction. This can be a positive aspect of this type of investing, because you'll be learning something new and stretching your mental and emotional muscles.

As in any alliance, the good has to outweigh the bad. You have to see some real *economic* benefits in investing with your spouse, lover, or friend. What are those benefits? They can be building a financial future, creating the opportunity for your kids to go to college, ridding yourself of financial worries, investing, or finding a good coach. If the partnership isn't working out for you—if it isn't moving you forward—then the gutsy thing to do is to make a new plan. Although you may be in a marriage or a relationship and wish, with your heart of hearts, that you could move forward financially with the person you love, if you see that it's not working, then you may have to set sail in your own ship and pursue a separate financial course.

I once met with a woman who had no financial plans or investments for her future. I'll call her Gail. Gail's husband, just forty-five years old, had suffered a heart attack. He was also overweight and diabetic. He had convinced himself that he wouldn't live much longer. He had an insurance policy, with Gail as the beneficiary. But for the moment, Gail was financially adrift. She was also emotionally drained by her husband's state of health. She hoped, of course, that he would survive his physical afflictions, but she knew that if he lived a normal life span, they were sure to have financial problems, since they had done nothing to ensure their future.

After much agonizing, Gail stepped up: She set her own financial path. She went to work, saved some of her salary, and used the savings to purchase a piece of rental property with her sister. The property is now an investment in Gail's Money Machine, which is growing so that it will give her cash flow in the future, no matter what happens.

The lesson to learn is that your investment decisions can't be driven by your heart. They must be securely planted in more pragmatic soil. Sometimes, the best thing to do when you love another is to stick by your standards and not compromise them, even when it means making choices he or she may not understand.

PARTNERING WITH YOUR MATE OR FRIEND

A financial partnership is a lot like sex: To get it right, you definitely need to talk about it.

We talked in Chapter 1 about how Americans talk more freely about sex than they do about money, and as a financial coach privy to family money secrets, I know it's true. A real financial partnership needs to start with a meeting of the minds, where you clearly identify and explore all the issues you'll need to resolve in order to embark on an investment program together. And this financial summit begins with a commitment that *there can't be any secrets*— and this includes secret *feelings* as well as facts.

Your understanding of your shared financial picture requires full disclosure on both sides. If there are assets in his name and you believe they should be in both your names, now is the time to make that change and be clear about how you feel they should be managed. If you consider your partner's investment philosophy too risky and gamelike, this is your chance to speak your mind about it—and then retool it together.

Is it uncomfortable for you to talk freely about money with your partner, or to ask the tough questions you know you should be asking? Many women feel that way. It may be helpful to conduct your financial summit meeting with the aid of an advocate—a financial planner or coach whom both of you respect and trust. A third party on hand can help defuse any tense moments that may arise and keep the discussion productive, nonjudgmental, and committed to full disclosure.

You remember Linette, who was wrestling with her financial future in the wake of a painful divorce. Living in her marriage was difficult on several levels—especially communication. There was none. Only after the breakup did Linette learn how Marshall had squandered much of their income and about the risky investments he had made. Most of the family assets had been listed in Marshall's name only; this had made it easier for him to conceal his activities from Linette. Fortunately, Linette's lawyer worked out a nice settlement for her during their divorce proceedings. Marshall will give her $55,000 in stock options and contribute monthly to the support of their daughter. The settlement helped jump-start Linette's sluggish Money Machine. Now she thinks her life could be much better. If she had known about the family finances all along and participated equally in the decision making, think of the heartache she would have avoided and the money saved.

Admittedly, open communication is something we often have to struggle to achieve. Here's how my husband, Ron, and I hone and maintain the communication skills that foster our fruitful partnership.

Ron and I make a concerted effort to talk a lot about our visions for our family, careers, and financial life—three spokes on our Wheel of Life. Sometimes these discussions last several days; it may take that long for our real feelings and real truths to emerge.

We've developed some great traditions that also help us maintain our openness and closeness. Each year on our wedding anniversary, we go to a quiet spot—a country inn or a remote resort—and have dinner at a nice romantic restaurant. We take turns planning this anniversary trip, and whoever designs the vacation keeps the details a secret from the other. That adds a little fun and makes it a big surprise. We won't even give a hint as to climate or activity! The mystified spouse has to try to guess by closely observing what the other packs: bathing suit and shorts, or heavy sweaters and jeans?

One year, I didn't get the clue! Guessing mountain experience, I had packed a warm quilted jacket and woolen dress for dinner. When we arrived in sunny Puerto Vallarta, Mexico, I had to rush down to the beach that night and buy one of those gauzy cotton dresses from a beach vendor. Of course, glitches like this just add to the sweet memories.

Once we reach our destination, we enjoy being together, and then the fun really begins. We traditionally have a Saturday night dinner, and each of us comes prepared with a list—hopefully, not too long a list!—of things we'd like to change in our marriage. We share our lists, and we each do our best to sit patiently and listen while the other person rattles off the personal list of requests, suggestions, observations, and challenges. The tricky part is not to be defensive.

One year, Ron's list included a request that I learn how to cook so I could make dinner once in a while. But I had never liked to cook—when I had a house built in Philadelphia, I asked the builder not to put in a kitchen! (He did, anyway.) But our annual tradition requires that we each honor the other's point of view—even when we find it difficult. So I honored Ron's request and went off to cooking school. I'm now a fairly competent chef, and nothing pleases me more than to share good food and good times with my husband, our family, and our friends.

Some years, our lists have included financial concerns. Ron thinks that we sometimes "put the cart before the horse" and need to slow down—that the *pressures* of life encourage us to move too fast and make financial decisions before we're really ready. I've often felt that way, too. Our annual talk gives us a chance to get issues like this onto the table and to make changes needed to keep the relationship fresh and satisfying.

The point is that when you take time to sit down with your partner in order to think about things, and you each have an opportunity to be truthful, it's amazing what you can learn and accomplish.

Here's another tradition we enjoy. Early in January, each year as a family, Ron, our son, Sean, and I find a quiet retreat away from the hustle and bustle of daily life and plan in the seven parts of our Wheel of Life. We ask ourselves what we have accomplished in each of the seven areas—family, social, career, mental, financial, physical, and spiritual—over the past year. We each make a chart, and we go around the table so that each family member can make a note about what's occurred in a specific area of life. Then we each make a second chart, this time noting the developments we'd like to see occur in each part of our lives. This really helps us learn about one another, too.

This shared exercise makes it pretty hard to ignore whether you're improving the financial part of your life—as well as all the others. Some wonderful goals and accomplishments have grown out of this family tradition: One year, writing this book had a prominent place on my chart.

There have been times when Ron and I found that we'd been distracted from focusing on the financial part of our lives. Other times, we realized that we'd neglected to create a common vision for our futures, or hadn't asked ourselves to maintain a higher standard of accomplishment so that our partnership could be stronger. Such oversights are okay; they happen in every relationship. Our annual Wheel of Life retreat provides a starting point for a discussion about who we are and how we are working together. Shortcomings can be addressed and remedied; successes can be celebrated. The place to begin in your relationship and life is wherever you are at the moment.

Planning Your First Money Talk

A partnership offers you an opportunity to get some honest feedback from someone who cares about who you are and where you're going. I think that's one of the main reasons that we form close relationships. It's no different in your money life. If you and your mate have not talked about what your financial picture looks like, *now* is the time to start.

Your first discussion about your financial partnership will lay the groundwork for your investment relationship, so it makes good sense to go into it with a written agenda, just as you would any important negotiation. An agenda will keep you sharp and focused, and it will keep you from feeling overwhelmed. Here are some issues and topics you might include:

- Taking an inventory of each partner's investment skills and deciding how each partner can be brought up to speed in any weak areas.
- Choosing an advocate for financial coaching.
- Setting ground rules for how an advocate will work with the partnership—for example, will it be acceptable for partners to meet individually with the advocate?
- Agreeing on a method for negotiating any disagreements about investment strategies.
- Investing individually rather than together when philosophical differences can't be reconciled.
- Changing the name(s) in which assets are held, if necessary.

- Making specific plans to expand the investments in your Money Machine.
- Deciding how investments will be monitored, and by whom.
- Agreeing on when and how the returns from the Money Machine may be used.
- Drafting wills, if necessary, or reviewing existing wills to make sure that they reflect your current situation and future plans.

These are the trees. But you'll also want to explore the forest—the larger vision you each have of your financial lives and your future:

- Are you creeping through credit card hell, living on plastic and paying high interest charges? If so, what steps will each of you take to change that picture?
- How do you both envision the future? Do you plan to stop working or to make a major change in your career at some point? If so, do you look forward to enjoying the same lifestyle as now or better?
- What assets are growing for you in your Money Machine? Will they provide the future income you need to live your dreams?
- What future responsibilities will you have beyond yourself (for example, supporting kids in school or a parent)?
- What needs to happen in your partnership so that you and your mate can live out the vision you both have? Do you both need to make compromises or changes?
- Do you both need to work out any issues about the future transfer of money to your mate, children, or other family members?

You may find that these topics prompt new discussions. Conversations on financial well-being will evolve much like the process of growing your Money Machine. As your crucial issues become resolved, the feeling of unease in your stomach will loosen up. My stepson, Sean, goes to a remarkable character-based prep school called the Hyde School, in Bath, Maine. Inside the doorway, a sign welcomes both parents and students alike with the following saying:

> THE TRUTH WILL SET YOU FREE . . . BUT FIRST IT WILL
> MAKE YOU MISERABLE.

This is no less true in our financial lives. Sometimes you will tackle tough issues. It may hurt. But you and your partner will find real freedom by airing these issues.

There's a real reason that sex is easier to talk about than money, even between intimate partners: When it comes to investments, there's no room for make-believe. There is room for romance, though. Taking a financial journey with someone else is a path of intimacy. But a woman should come to the table fully equipped with a knowledge of all her options and her own set of fully defined investment goals. Thus prepared, you and your partner may find that by formulating, implementing, and tracking your plans, you're having the time of your lives and developing bonds more intimate than ever before.

June feels more connected with her husband ever since they began talking about their money life. She called the other day and told me that her husband had surprised her with a long weekend at a romantic little inn on Michigan's Upper Peninsula. They hadn't been away, alone, for nearly eighteen years. In fact, money talk—and the deeper talk about goals, dreams, wishes, and plans that money talk naturally opens—has broadened their intimacy and unveiled a whole new and spirited realm of conversation for them.

PARTNERING WITH AN INVESTMENT CLUB

Another way to benefit from a financial partnership is to join an association, like an investment club, where a group of people pool their money and ideas and invest together.

According to the National Association of Investors Corporation (NAIC), the parent organization of the investment club movement, there are over seventeen thousand investment clubs in the United States. They include women-only clubs, men-only clubs, and mixed organizations; members range from teenagers to octogenarians. Women in particular are catching the investment club bug. From high-profile professionals in New York City to those wonderful Beardstown Ladies in Illinois—the Beardstown Ladies have written their own best-selling investment guides—women are coming together with the same premise: A group can be a bridge to making powerful and profitable financial and wealth-building decisions, and it can inspire people to take charge of their own money lives.

An investment club presents a forum in which all questions regarding money matters are fair game. Members meet, usually monthly, to share investment ideas, to report on companies whose stock they are considering buying, and to make joint investment decisions. Sometimes investment experts or other outside guests are invited to give talks or answer questions.

Investment club members may be of modest means or prosperous. The women of the 008 Club in New York City represent one extreme: They are well positioned in their jobs and married to financially successful men. But they formed the club because they believed that they had a real need, as women, to learn more about money, and they publicly acknowledged how little they knew about how to make it work for them. The Beardstown Ladies are superficially different: They are mostly high school graduates, and many are not professionals. However, they reached the same conclusion about their need for financial know-how. Through commitment and dedication, both groups have produced astounding financial results for their members.

The investment club phenomenon demonstrates once again that women have the right stuff to be great investors. From 1985 to 1994, according to the NAIC, all-women clubs earned a higher annual investment return than all-men clubs in seven out of ten years.

I recently had the good fortune to meet the Beardstown Ladies.

Several of their members were speaking at Tony Robbins's Financial Mastery seminar—to which all of us at my firm, Take Charge Financial!, look forward to going each year to be financial coaches. (The program is a hoot. It offers lots of good times to go along with financial learning.) Since I, too, am a midwesterner, I felt right at home with the Beardstown Ladies; talking with them was like talking with my own grandmother, aunt, or sister. I was so touched by their genuineness.

At one point during the seminar, Tony spins a big prize wheel to give away various goodies. The year I met the Beardstown Ladies, one of the oldest members of their group won the grand prize—a Harley-Davidson motorcycle. She hopped right on the bike and posed for pictures.

I shared dinner with the Ladies one night, and we reminisced about growing up in the Midwest—Beardstown is only a stone's throw from where I grew up in central Illinois. In a very sweet way, they were obviously relishing their newfound celebrity—even while being a bit awed by it—and their status as models of investment success for women—and men, too.

The Beardstown Ladies aren't alone. A majority of investment clubs outperform the Dow Jones Industrial Average in a given year. However, joining a club is not going to automatically solve all your financial needs and concerns. Up to 40 percent of new investment clubs fold in less than two years, usually because members are not committed to spending the time and energy that is required to create a thriving club.

One of the associates in our office is a member of an investment club that is not operating up to its potential. She's frustrated by belonging to an organization that has only a few members who dig in and go for it. Many in her club sit back, clinging to the same belief that sent them to an investment club to begin with: They don't know about all this "investing stuff" and it's too difficult to learn, so someone else can do it for them. These people will have to change their attitudes, develop some enthusiasm, and get committed to tackling the challenges of wealth building, or they will continue to diminish the opportunity for the rest of the members to do so and will ultimately doom the club.

It's easy to form an investment club or join an existing one. The rules and guidelines are contained in the club bylaws, which specify the yearly or monthly contribution expected from each member, the schedule of meetings, attendance requirements, and the financial arrangements that apply when you join or leave the club. Most bylaws also tell you about the club's policy for buying and selling stock, and the procedure for electing officers. You'll certainly want to read the bylaws of any club you are thinking of joining. The NAIC publishes lots of material, including an investment manual. This information can help you form your own club.

While clubs often meet monthly and require that members chip in from $20 to $50 or more a month to the club's investment account, others may have very different guidelines. Maybe you'll want to start an investment club with people you know are really committed to growing their Money Machines and to ensuring their financial futures. You could meet weekly, and you could each contribute 10 percent of your salaries. That way, you would be making your investment club a central focus of your Money Machine.

Maggie, our friend from New Orleans, joined an investment club that meets every two weeks. Their selection committee scopes out good mutual funds and stocks and presents them to the group for investment consideration. They discuss each proposed stock or mutual fund (the group has stayed away from bonds) and then decide which ones to choose for their portfolio. Then one person acts as a liaison between the group and its broker and authorizes the actual investment.

At one meeting, Maggie told the group about a new film-developing technique she had learned about at her job. The company holding the patent had always been at the cutting edge of photography and film. Maggie suggested that the group might want to consider buying a small amount of the company's stock. After further research into the company's finances and management, the group agreed to do so, and Maggie's advice turned out to be a winner. The club saw the stock rise by two points in the first week they owned it!

An investment club can be a valuable element of your investment picture. Chances are that your investment club portfolio won't contain your whole Money Machine; in fact, the NAIC reports that most investment club members build their own individual investment portfolios, even while they enjoy the benefits of club participation.

Finding a good investment club might take a little research. Clubs vary in their effectiveness and methods. Some clubs are more serious than others about educating their members; some make larger investment commitments than others; some are better organized than others; and some have produced better financial results for a longer period of time. Get to know the members of a club you're thinking of joining before you sign up. Make sure you have compatible interests and investment philosophies. Ask yourself: Does the club have a mission? Are its members dedicated to this mission? Then see if that mission fits yours. If you're serious, you're not looking for dabblers because you don't have time in your own life to dabble, and particularly not in one of the major areas of your Wheel of Life.

Whether you invest with a knowledgeable partner or a good club, investing with others is a great learning opportunity. It's like tennis or any other sport: If you can play with athletes who are better than you, you'll be challenged to improve your game.

On a windy, sun-filled day, I returned to Rancho La Puerta. It had been an entire year since the "hot-tub confab," and I looked forward to seeing women I had come to know, understand, and care about.

I rode across the border from San Diego with a sense of excitement, and when we finally pulled into the plaza in front of the retreat's main entrance, I bounced happily from the bus. While the luggage was being unloaded, I strolled down a walk laden with vines and fragrant flowers to the dining hall so that I could have a light lunch.

"Joan!" called a familiar voice. I turned to see Sadie Chung sitting at a large table on the back patio. We hugged, and after going inside to fill my tray with salad, minestrone soup, and some delicious seven-grain bread, I joined her.

Sadie looked wonderful. Her skin had a fresh-washed glow that made her appear much younger than her sixty years. Her face had lost much of its puffiness, and her forehead wasn't quite as crinkled with worry as it had been a year earlier.

"I heard you're writing a book," she said.

"Yes," I replied. "It will be out next year."

"What's it all about?"

"Women and money," I said. "Actually, the book was born right here at the Ranch. Remember that evening last year when we first met? We shared a hot tub with five other women?"

"Of course, dear," Sadie said. "That conversation really had quite an influence on me, and it inspired some changes. You know, until we met, I was going to stop traveling, playing bridge, entertaining, just about everything except the volunteer work I do—all because my money was such a mess. You inspired me and you helped me 'clean out my closet,' so to speak, and left me with time for the things I really love."

"Thank you so much, Sadie. I'm glad I could help you, and I hope my book will bring the same message to other women, too," I said.

Later that night, Sadie and I met for dinner. We found our old table near the open hearth and greeted old friends as they walked by. I spotted a pregnant woman walking arm in arm with a young, attractive man.

"Rachel! Please join us," I said with glee.

Rachel and her husband, David, were beginning to fill us in on their year when June breezed in. She had an energy and a spring to her stride, and an air of confidence that simply hadn't existed a year ago.

"I haven't kept still for two weeks straight!" June announced. "Steve and I are on the go all the time, and my mother is even taking a few trips every now and then."

Not only had June made some smart choices for her and Steve's money, but she had also proven to be a good manager of her mother's cash. At the age of seventy-three, her mother needed a nice return on the dollar to produce a good, steady income. So June took $100,000 from her father's insurance policy and put it into several sturdy mutual funds. She put the other $25,000 in some Treasury notes, which mature every six months, in case her mother needs money to take care of emergencies, or wants some extra cash to splurge on herself.

Steve, as it turns out, is very happy with June's newfound financial savvy. "He's real proud of me," June said. "I thought he'd pull that *man* thing about being the provider and the money manager. But he was relieved, I think, to be able to step aside—or stand by me—so we could do this together. We're partners now."

"That's just great," I said.

"Yes, June, it is. I guess all of us made some changes over the year." Rachel beamed.

That was David's cue. "I don't know if Rachel told you, Joan, but we had delayed having a child because we both were afraid we wouldn't be able to afford one."

"We feel so relieved now, knowing that our financial future is progressing," Rachel jumped in. "I'm telling you, there's nothing like peace of mind. *Nothing.*"

Our little group was shaping up for a reunion, but we were missing a few of our hot-tub companions. Betty and Linette were late, but would be there for sure.

Maggie, though, would not be coming. I had talked to her shortly before Christmas, and she said the retreat was not in her budget this year. She'd started working a number of craft fairs, selling her handmade photo frames. She was doing so well that her second job was beginning to eclipse her primary one. But she remained at the photographer's studio because of its health and insurance benefits, which would be too costly for her to assume on her own.

From our conversation, I could tell that Maggie, too, had changed during the year. She'd grown more mature and more certain of herself. And the sweetest part is that Maggie and her mother have a closer, more adult relationship. They've been helping each other to understand their money lives better, and Patricia has even joined Maggie's investment club.

We all missed not having Maggie around, but Betty with her quick wit, and Linette with her infectious good nature, filled in the gap. They missed our dinner because they'd been delayed at the airport, but Linette was waiting for me in my room when I returned later that evening. Her eyes sparkled, and the red rim left from a trail of tears was no more.

"Kimberly and I are doing real well," Linette said. "I hated leaving her for a week, but my mother was delighted to have her all to herself. When I was married, we always had a nanny stay over when we went away. But you know something? I don't miss it in the least." We sat curled on the soft cotton rug before the fireplace as we sipped from mugs of hot cider.

"You seem much more peaceful," I said.

"The divorce is final, and I feel terrific, mostly because *I'm* in charge of me now, not Marshall. I know where my money is going, and I know where I'm going. It feels great," she said.

Using the $55,000 in stock options she got in the divorce, Linette opened her own brokerage account and, with the help of a good coach, made more intelligent investment choices than Marshall had by choosing three wave-of-the-future mutual funds. Her Money Machine is now steaming. She also rents out the beach house for part of the year, and the income helps pay for Kimberly's schooling.

My companions were walking easier and brighter paths in their lives, and I was touched by the great strides they had taken and the courage they'd shown.

The next morning, I went hiking up the mountain with Betty. Once again, we were awed by the dramatic colors early morning brings, and we drank in the sweet rosemary-laced air. As we neared "the pig," that jagged touchstone that marked the highest point of our journey, Betty turned to me and announced she had something important to tell me. "But I'd better wait until we're back down the mountain," she added mischievously. "You'll be so surprised, you might trip and fall!"

She broke the news as we crossed the footbridge leading back to the Ranch. "I quit my job," she said with a grin. "Now I just work part-time as a consultant. I made a little studio in my basement, and I started making pots. I also held my very first mentoring session with a few girls at a high school in Oakland."

"Betty, how fabulous! Congratulations! But how does your stomach feel?" I asked.

"Calm as a clam. I couldn't be happier. And you know what? Although I'm working part-time, I'm still generating enough income to pay my mortgage and meet my necessities, *plus* feed my Money Machine," she said. "It's a dream come true."

A friendly breeze brushed by us as we paused by a tree, stretching and breathing deeply to cool our bodies and let our hearts slow down to their normal pace. The wind captured the rosemary scent. We could tell it was going to be a beautiful day.

Ah, such sweet pleasure!

Women hold up half the sky.

—ANONYMOUS

Advocate: Someone you've chosen to coach you in enhancing your financial well-being. An advocate can provide a variety of financial services, including helping you to create the best possible strategies for consistently investing your cash and improving the growth of your Money Machine. See also *Broker* and *Financial Adviser.*

Annuity: An investment that shelters from taxation any profit you make on your mutual funds but does not shelter you from paying taxes when you withdraw money. An annuity is an expensive way to convert capital gains into ordinary income when you're ready to withdraw your money. Like an IRA, an annuity ties up your cash until age fifty-nine and a half.

Bear Market: Yahoo! Stock prices are falling. This means that stocks are "on sale." It's a buyer's market and a good climate for the long-term investor.

Blue-Chip Stock: A stock representing a large, well-known company that has a long history of consistent corporate earnings. Blue chips include companies like IBM, General Electric, General Motors, and Kodak.

Bond: A security that pays you interest for a specified period and then repays you the face value of the security at the end of that time. Types of bonds include certificates of deposit (CDs), government savings bonds, Treasury notes and bonds, mortgage-backed bonds, municipal bonds, and corporate bonds. Bonds vary by issuer, time span, and rate of return. If you own a bond, you're a creditor of the issuer. By contrast, if you're a stockholder, you're an owner.

Broker: An advocate who has direct access to the trading floor of securities exchanges and the over-the-counter market. Brokers buy and sell stocks, bonds, and mutual funds for you for a commission. A broker must be licensed by the NASD. See also *Advocate.*

Brokerage Account: An investment account in your name (or jointly with another person). A brokerage account is like a checking account, except that a brokerage account is held at a brokerage firm rather than a bank. Also unlike a checking account, a brokerage account may contain both cash and securities. Cash in a brokerage account may be kept in a money market fund to collect interest; when you choose, it may be used to purchase stocks, mutual funds, or other investments within your same account. As with a checking account, you will receive a monthly statement showing what's held in your account.

Bull Market: Yahoo! Stock prices are rising.

Capital Gain: When you buy a stock, a mutual fund, or real estate for one price and sell it later for a higher price, the difference (your profit) is called a "capital gain" for tax purposes. Historically, tax rates on capital gains have been lower than tax rates on regular income. You are required to declare a capital gain on your tax return only if your investment is in File Cabinet No. 1 (taxable investments).

Capital Loss: When you buy a stock, a mutual fund, or real estate for one price and sell it at a lower price, the difference is called a "capital loss" for tax purposes. You record a capital loss on your tax return only if your investment is in File Cabinet No. 1, because File Cabinets No. 2 and No. 3 exempt you from taxes at this point. You can use a capital loss in File Cabinet No. 1 to offset other capital gains in this cabinet. Example: If you made some money in Microsoft stock but lost some in GM, you can offset one with the other. See also *File Cabinet No. 1, File Cabinet No. 2,* and *File Cabinet No. 3.*

Cash Value: The amount of money invested in an insurance policy. Under tax laws, you can borrow the cash value of a policy, usually anytime after the first year of the policy. Just like money borrowed from a bank, money borrowed against an insurance policy doesn't have any tax liability.

Certificate of Deposit: Also known as a CD, a certificate issued to you by a bank for a deposit that cannot be withdrawn for months or even years. The low rate of interest doesn't keep you ahead of inflation and taxes or build your Money Machine.

Common Stock: A share of ownership in a company. As an owner, you typically elect a board of directors, whose duties include issuing dividends. If the company dissolves for any reason, common stockholders will be the last in line to receive assets.

Death Benefit: The amount of dollars that will go tax free to those you have named in an insurance policy to receive these funds upon your death. There may be estate taxes, depending upon your estate planning.

Debit Card: A piece of plastic that looks and functions much like a Visa or a MasterCard. You may use it to purchase groceries, rent a car, buy an airline ticket, order from a catalog, or do anything else that you can with a credit card. The difference is that instead of building up debt, your purchases are deducted from your bank account so that you're always spending your own money.

Dignity Money: The amount of cash you'll need each year from your Money Machine to pay for basics, like housing, transportation, food, and taxes.

Discount Broker: A broker who buys and sells whatever you request (stocks, bonds, mutual funds) but does not advise you about your purchase or your financial life. The transaction charges of a discount broker are lower than those of an advocate.

Dividend: A share of the profits of a company in which you hold stock. You may receive dividends either quarterly or annually.

Dow Jones Industrial Average: Also known as the Dow, it is a way to measure the growth of the price of stocks in the United States by examining the prices of the same thirty stocks each day. The Dow plots the rise and fall of these stocks as they are bought and sold, thereby using them as a mirror of the market. Consider the Dow a weather vane of sorts: It heralds the ups and downs of Wall Street.

Education IRA: A new form of IRA that allows you to contribute up to $500 a year for each child until the child's eighteenth birthday. When the child reaches age thirty, the Education IRA reverts to a Plus IRA. (See also *Roth IRA.*)

File Cabinet No. 1:   Investments that are taxed across the board. This file cabinet represents stocks, bonds and real estate investments where after-tax dollars go into them, and earnings and profits are taxed.

File Cabinet No. 2:   In this file cabinet, you're spared some tax on your investments because it represents "qualified plans" such as IRAs, 401(k) plans, etc. Tax-free dollars go into File Cabinet No. 2, and earnings from stocks, bonds, and real estate grow tax free. When you withdraw money from this file cabinet, you'll be taxed at your ordinary income tax rate. If your combined state and federal tax rate is 50 percent, half of everything you have in this file cabinet is Uncle Sam's.

File Cabinet No. 3:   You're spared even more tax on your investments in this file cabinet. This represents the private pension plan. In this case, you've already paid tax on dollars that go into stocks, bonds, or real estate. Earnings and profits from stocks, bonds, and real estate investments are tax free. And, most notably, you can withdraw your money from these investments tax free.

Financial Adviser: An advocate who charges you a fee, usually quarterly or yearly, to help you build your financial wealth. A financial adviser must be licensed under state laws and associated with a firm that can buy and sell securities. See also *Advocate.*

Flexible Premium Variable Life Insurance Plan: Variable insurance combined with good mutual funds to work as an investment plan for your money. To work as an investment, the plan has to have low term-insurance rates, guaranteed interest rates to withdraw your money, and mutual funds that have a history of performing as well as the stock market. See also *Private Pension Plan.*

401(k) Plan: Named after a section in the U.S. tax code, a 401(k) plan is a company-sponsored qualified plan in which you allow your employer to regularly deduct money from your paycheck tax free and invest the money in stocks, bonds, or real estate. Your investments grow tax free, but you are taxed at your ordinary income tax rate when you withdraw the funds. Your employer may match your contribution to some extent. These moneys are tied up until you're fifty-nine and a half, unless you want to pay a penalty for withdrawing your money early of 10 percent plus the ordinary income tax due. 401(k) plans are not federally insured. See also *Qualified Plan.*

Growth Mutual Fund: A mutual fund composed of stocks in companies that will grow faster than the economy. This kind of fund usually doesn't pay much in dividends. Also see *Mutual Fund.*

Individual Retirement Account (IRA): A qualified plan that allows you to make an annual tax-free contribution of up to $2,000. Investments in your IRA grow tax free. Your money is tied up until you're fifty-nine and a half, unless you want to pay a 10 percent penalty plus the tax for withdrawing your money early. IRAs are federally insured. See also *Qualified Plan.* New tax-law legislation created two circumstances in which you can withdraw money before age fifty-nine and a half without a penalty. These are for your child's education and to purchase your first home. But you still must pay income tax on the withdrawal.

International Mutual Fund: A mutual fund composed of stocks in foreign companies, like telephone companies in Mexico, health-care companies in Europe, and manufacturing companies in China. See also *Mutual Fund.*

Keogh Plan: A qualified plan that allows you to make an annual tax-free contribution of up to 20 percent of your earnings or $30,000, whichever is less, and invest the money. Like IRAs and 401(k) plans, the money grows tax free, but it is taxed at your ordinary income-tax rate upon withdrawal. These monies are tied up until you're fifty-nine and a half, unless you want to pay a 10 percent penalty plus the tax for withdrawing the money early. See also *Qualified Plan.*

Marginal Tax Rate: The highest federal tax rate that you can be charged on some part of your income.

Money Machine: That well-oiled piece of machinery that houses all of your investments while they grow. It is the lifeblood of your future. It is the generator of all future cash and what you will need in order to create and lead a healthy, stress-free, and joyful life. Think of it as a pot of invested capital that is sufficient to create the income that will meet your future lifestyle expenses and your financial goals.

Money Market Fund: A fund for your short-term needs. A money market fund pays you interest from the short-term debt obligations of various companies. Brokerage firms usually have higher interest rates on their money market funds than banks and credit unions.

Municipal Bond: Debt incurred by cities, counties, and states to gather cash in order to build public projects, like roads, schools, football stadiums, airports, sewer and water systems, hospitals, public housing, theaters, redevelopment projects, public parking, environmental control and safety projects, and government buildings. Much as you can have a mortgage on a house, a city, county, or state has a mortgage on its property; the municipality pays interest on the borrowed money. When you are a municipal bond holder, you have lent your money for projects, and you receive interest that is tax free. At the stated maturity of the bond, you are repaid. See also *Bond.*

Mutual Fund (Stocks): A bundle of stocks. A mutual fund allows you to own a piece of many companies instead of only one. Mutual funds vary in focus: Some are composed of high-tech stocks, others of health-care stocks, international stocks, or blue chips. A mutual fund has a professional manager, who buys for and sells from the fund's portfolio.

Mutual Fund Family: Mutual funds can exist in a family, often as individual members with distinctive personalities sharing a common last name. Some mutual fund families contain as many as two hundred funds; some have as few as twenty. If you invest in a family and decide that you want to be in one of its funds rather than another, you can generally move within the family at no cost.

NASD: The National Association of Securities Dealers. A self-regulatory body overseen by the Securities and Exchange Commission (SEC). The NASD watches the operations and ethics of its licensed securities brokers and dealers. It can sanction and fine members who do not abide by its rules and regulations. In order to provide brokerage services, all individuals and firms must be registered with the NASD.

NASDAQ: A communications system developed by the NASD for exchanging over-the-counter quotes among the members of the NASD.

Net Asset Value: The total shares divided into the total market value, less any liabilities, of a mutual fund's securities. The commission paid to buy the fund is generally the difference between the fund's share price and the NAV.

No-Load: A stock or mutual fund that can be purchased without paying a commission or a sales charge. The administration of the fund includes other management costs and fees.

NYSE: The New York Stock Exchange, in lower Manhattan, is where buyers and sellers of stocks get together to establish a price for their trades. The NYSE is one of the three major exchanges (the other two are the American Stock Exchange and the Pacific Stock Exchange). For every "buy" on these exchanges there is a matching "sell," thereby creating a fluid market.

Ordinary Income: A year's income that is taxed according to ordinary federal and state income-tax rates.

OTC: The over-the-counter market is a negotiation between dealers throughout the United States for the purchase and sale of stocks. Unlike the NYSE, a "buy" is not always matched to a "sell." A dealer may buy some stock and hold it in inventory. Thus, the dealer, instead of a third-party buyer, establishes the price. In the OTC, prices of stock may vary widely from one dealer's offer to another. Price differences often depend on how the dealer plans to profit on the stock.

Price/Earnings (P/E) Ratio: A stock's price divided by its earnings per share for the prior year. This shows how much people are willing to pay for ownership of $1 of the company's earnings.

Private Pension Plan (PPP): Also known as a flexible premium variable life insurance plan, the PPP takes advantage of the best of what insurance has to offer (the ability to grow money tax free and withdraw it tax free) and the best of what the stock market (the historically best way to grow money) has to offer. Unlike with qualified plans, Uncle Sam is not your partner when you withdraw money from a PPP. See also *Flexible Premium Variable Life Insurance Plan.*

Qualified Plan: A plan that by special tax law allows you to invest and grow money tax free. You'll pay taxes at your ordinary income-tax rate when you withdraw your money. And there is a 10 percent penalty plus the tax for withdrawing cash before you are fifty-nine and a half. Qualified plans include IRAs, SEP-IRAs, Keogh plans, 401(k) plans, 403 (b) plans, company pension plans, and profit-sharing plans. There is a limit on how much money you can put into a qualified plan each year, depending upon which plan you use.

Regular Account: A brokerage account that is fully taxed; interest, dividends, and gains on the sales of securities are taxable income for state and federal tax purposes.

Roth IRA: This new provision allows you to contribute up to $2,000 a year to your Roth IRA. Under the new legislation, you won't have a tax deduction for your contributions, but you will be able to withdraw tax free. If you earn over $95,000 a year or if you and your spouse jointly earn over $150,000, you can't use this IRA. Also known as the American Dream IRA and the Plus IRA.

Rule of 72:   A simple mathematical formula that lets you project the growth of your Money Machine and the income you'll be seeing in the future. To apply the rule, divide the number 72 by a rate of return. The result is the number of years your money will take to double at that particular rate. To get the rate of interest you'll need to reach your financial goal, divide the number of years you plan to double your money into the number 72.

Securities Investor Protection Corporation (SIPC):   A federally chartered nonprofit membership corporation that protects customer accounts of brokers who have financial difficulties. Under the SIPC, brokerage accounts are insured up to $500,000 per account.

Simple IRA: A qualified plan in which employees of small companies can both invest money themselves and/or have their employer make contributions to the IRA. It works the same way as a traditional IRA by taxing you at your regular income-tax rate when you withdraw money. As an employee, you can make contributions to your simple IRA of up to $6,000 a year. The employer must either elect to contribute a flat 2 percent of the employee's yearly salary or match the employee's contributions dollar for dollar to a maximum of 3 percent of the employee's salary or $6,000, whichever is less. You can have a simple IRA and at the same time contribute to a traditional IRA. However, the amount of your contribution that may be tax deductible will depend upon your income.

Simplified Employee Pension–Individual Retirement Account (SEP-IRA):   A qualified plan that lets you (if you're self-employed) invest up to $30,000 a year or 15 percent of your annual earned income, whichever is less, and your investments grow tax free. When you withdraw money from a SEP-IRA, you'll pay taxes at your ordinary income-tax rate. These monies are tied up until you're fifty-nine and a half unless you want to pay a 10 percent penalty plus the tax for withdrawing your money early. See also *Qualified Plan.*

Small Cap Mutual Fund: A mutual fund composed of stocks in companies that have a lot of room to grow. Apple, Applied Materials, and the Gap were all small cap stocks at one time. Now, though, they have grown beyond small cap distinction. Historically, small cap stocks have been the best performers in the stock market because they have the potential to grow bigger. See also *Mutual Fund.*

Stock: Ownership in a company that is traded either on a national exchange, like the NYSE, or simply between individuals. A stock represents a piece of ownership in a company.

Tax-Exempt Income: Income you receive that is not subject to federal or state taxes.

Term Insurance: Life insurance that pays a death benefit for a specific period. Term insurance is renewable. Term insurance is the least expensive form of insurance.

Value Mutual Fund: A mutual fund composed of stocks in companies that are fully grown but for one reason or another undervalued by the market. At times, the stock of IBM, Hewlett-Packard, and Citibank have all been "cheap" compared to their value. Managers of value funds look for these bargains and expect the prices of these stocks to rise. See also *Mutual Fund.*

White Knight Syndrome: The notion that women need and sometimes expect someone to take care of them. It is the false idea that you don't have to worry about your financial life because your husband, boyfriend, father, domestic partner, or someone else will take care of you and see to your every need, and you'll never, ever have to worry. It is a condition that has single-handedly made a vast number of women financial cripples, a belief system that prevents women from moving forward, taking control of their own destinies, and realizing their well-being and security.

Whole Life Insurance: Life insurance with level premiums, level death benefits, and cash value. Whole life is not a good investment for your Money Machine. It is a more expensive form of insurance than term insurance.

HOW TO CONTACT THE AUTHOR

You are invited to contact the author with your questions and experiences in applying the concepts in this book to your own financial life, or to obtain information on the following:

- "A Girl Needs Cash" seminars
- Company or organization programs
- Workbook materials
- Other programs and material available from Take Charge Financial!

And please visit our website at www.TAKECHARGEFIN.com.

Please provide telephone, fax, and e-mail information with your name and address.

Address correspondence to:

Joan Perry
Take Charge Financial!
315 University Avenue
Los Gatos, CA 95030

fax: 408-399-6606
e-mail: info@takechargefin.com